ENVIRONMENTAL
HISTORY
of
LAKE TAHOE

ENVIRONMENTAL
HISTORY
of
LAKE TAHOE

DAVID C. ANTONUCCI

AMERICA
THROUGH TIME®
ADDING COLOR TO AMERICAN HISTORY

For all those who love Lake Tahoe and strive tirelessly to preserve its virtues for future generations.

America Through Time is an imprint of Fonthill Media LLC
www.through-time.com
office@through-time.com

Published by Arcadia Publishing by arrangement with Fonthill Media LLC
For all general information, please contact Arcadia Publishing:
Telephone: 843-853-2070
Fax: 843-853-0044
E-mail: sales@arcadiapublishing.com
For customer service and orders:
Toll-Free 1-888-313-2665

www.arcadiapublishing.com

First published 2022

Copyright © David C. Antonucci 2022

ISBN 978-1-63499-417-0

Typeset in Mrs Eaves XL Serif Narrow
Printed and bound in England

CONTENTS

Pondering Tahoe from the Tahoe Rim Trail
by Jenny Antonucci.

PREFACE

As a young civil and environmental engineer, I worked for the Lahontan Regional Water Quality Control Board, the water pollution control agency for a large region of eastern California that included Lake Tahoe's California side. At age twenty-four, they promoted me to Lake Tahoe, a mere sixteen months into my career, in January 1975. My new job was to oversee the enforcement of new water pollution laws at Lake Tahoe and other Northeastern California watersheds.

I previously studied Lake Tahoe and analyzed the South Lake Tahoe wastewater treatment plant as my master's report for a graduate degree in civil and environmental engineering. I had visited the lake a few times, once at age eleven, again as part of a college class and made occasional short trips for the Water Board.

Even so, as I began my new position, I understood little about the natural and political environments of Tahoe. I was soon to learn a lot about both and learn it extremely fast. Russell Culp, a highly respected civil and environmental engineer at Tahoe, warned me to be on the lookout for "political buzz saws," of which there were many. I would add to this the regulatory trap doors, developer leghold traps, and environmentalist land mines.

The central pragmatic question that struck me was, "How did we get to this point and why?" Often, I found myself defending strict regulatory actions to undo the damage of others' past misdeeds, as judged by modern standards. Understanding Lake Tahoe's interconnected human and environmental history was critical to grasping the current situation and avoiding past mistakes.

My quest began to determine what constituted reality, interpret it, and present it as fact-based knowledge. What was unique about this process was that Tahoe's past events often crossed the rare intersection of history, science, and politics. This book initially started as a chapter of a comprehensive book on Lake Tahoe's natural history and science. However, I quickly realized the subject was more complex than what one could explain in just one chapter.

My goal is to enlighten those who care about Lake Tahoe's future. Thus, after all these years, I wrote this book to explain and interpret Tahoe's past and present. I hope you will appreciate learning about this critical facet of Lake Tahoe's rich history as much as I enjoyed discovering it.

In the interest of full disclosure, I was a witness and participant in the controversies, plans, projects, and decisions between 1975 and 2021. These appear in Chapters 9 and 10. As such, I have tried to be impartial and consistent, but I will let the reader be a judge of that.

If you are wondering how to read this book, follow these suggested paths. If you are already familiar with the events and impacts during late-nineteenth and early-twentieth century Tahoe history, go to the contents, determine the era you want to start with, locate its beginning page, and read from there. If you are not familiar with early Tahoe human history, review Figure 1 to get the "big picture" of the flow of events and begin reading with the introduction.

Many thanks and much appreciation to Dr. David Borges, Scott Hackley, Tim Hauserman, and Carol Jensen for their careful review and beneficial critique of the manuscript's early and very rough drafts.

This book is organic; updates will occur as Tahoe's human and environmental history continues to unfold. Visit the website TahoeFacts.com for updates and more information on Lake Tahoe.

David C. Antonucci

David C. Antonucci
Tahoma, California

INTRODUCTION

The story of Lake Tahoe is the story of people and the environment and their reciprocal influences. The environment shaped the lives of early people of Tahoe, and recent people shaped the Tahoe environment. Native peoples, pioneers, and early visitors conformed to the environment's demands and existed in harmony with their surroundings. By 1860, loggers, hoteliers, ranchers, developers, and tourists imposed their demands on Tahoe's resources, forever changing it for the generations that followed. Early on, the motivation for resource exploitation for personal benefit prevailed but then collided with and became subordinate to rising beliefs in the preservation and appreciation of our natural resources.

This book's title, *The Environmental History of Lake Tahoe*, encapsulates Lake Tahoe's intertwined human and environmental histories as a three-act ecological drama with good and bad actors. In the first act, the Native American people and early pioneers benignly inhabit the Tahoe Basin. The second act witnesses the Euro-Americans' eviction of Native Americans, seizure of timber, land, and water combined with the unsustainable uses of these resources for individual and corporate benefit. The third act is the ongoing resolution of conflict and movement to collaboration. In the closing scene of the third act, stakeholders accept that Tahoe exists for all and deserves to continue as a resource preserved for the common good and managed for long-term sustainability.

Presenting the history of Lake Tahoe's human and environmental precedents is more than just a recitation of the chronology of acts of various occupiers and the resulting changes to the environment. It seeks to connect us intimately with the past, respect and clarify the legacies of the individuals who came before us, and describe how we became who and what we are today. By helping us understand our past, an objective human and environmental history unifies us socially and across generations while making us more proficient in anticipating our future.

A relentless undercurrent throughout modern Tahoe events is the undeniable principle that the ability of technologically sophisticated humans to change the environment exceeds their ability to foresee and concern themselves with the impacts of these changes. Loggers plundered the forests over four decades in the middle to late nineteenth century. Early twentieth-century government policy mandating wildfire suppression caused the ravaged woodland to evolve into an unhealthy condition that triggered stress, disease, and greater wildfire danger. Fishery biologists planted game fish and microscopic Mysis shrimp in the lake that resulted in a partial collapse of the aquatic ecosystem and contributed to the local extinction of a native species. Intense construction of roads, housing, commercial structures, and ski areas over forty years disturbed the stable watershed and natural flood-plains. These actions caused erosion and polluted runoff to enter the lake and decreased its clarity for generations.

Beginning with the Euro-American occupation and continuing to this day, a theme of conflict recurred. The conflict between individual human benefit and the broader societal interests weaved its way through the Tahoe historical narrative. This theme is the "Tahoe Conflict"—the battle over the opportunity to conserve and protect the natural gifts of Tahoe for the long-term public good or to exploit its natural resources for short-term individual and corporate benefit, and secondarily for societal progress. Over history, the Tahoe Conflict skirmishes play out repeatedly but only begin to resolve in the late twentieth century.

The Tahoe Conflict is the real-life enactment of ecologist Garrett Hardin's "Tragedy of the Commons." In Hardin's venerable fable, individual shepherds who graze a common pasture at capacity face whether to add one more animal to their herd. If they add that one additional animal, they benefit solely. Still, all shepherds suffer the loss of profit from the overgrazing it causes. The problem it creates is the conflict over individual benefit versus community wellbeing and sustainability. Metaphorically, the historical answer at Tahoe has always been to add that one new grazing animal. The general society, represented by the other shepherds, suffered the consequences and forced them to accept the lessened productivity resulting from the broadly ill effects of overgrazing.

Understanding and accepting the environmental history of Lake Tahoe ensures we have learned from our past and resolved to not repeat our missteps here or in any other area of ecological significance. It is worth emulating elsewhere the Lake Tahoe land-use regulation and lake protection model of (a) mandatory coordinated, consistent and compliant plan-ning across all political boundaries under oversight by a single regionwide agency, (b) an all-encompassing approach within natural resource boundaries, (c) environment, economy and community interests folded into all solutions, and (d) science and fact-based decision making. Indeed, many national and international parties look to Lake Tahoe as a source of cutting-edge environmental research and as an example of what can be accomplished through cooperation among all stakeholders.

1

Historical Eras of People and the Tahoe Environment

Visualize a soaring old-growth forest, clear running streams teeming with spawning cutthroat trout, plentiful growths of edible plants, and peaceful villages of cooperative inhabitants. The Native Americans acquiesced to the power of the natural environment. Winter snowfall drove them from the Tahoe Basin. They relied on organic sources for food by gathering available plants, hunting wildlife, or carrying in food from other areas. Starvation was always a possibility when natural resources became depleted or unavailable due to drought. If wildfire erupted, they abandoned their settlements and evacuated to safer locations. They relied on native materials to construct their shelter using only rudimentary tools and techniques to assemble a structure.

This idyllic scene gives way to rapacious loggers who plunder the forest within forty years, leaving a barren landscape of smoldering devastation and a polluted lake.

In the fifty or so years following, Tahoe followed a low-impact tourism model in a national park style. Land and water mass transportation modes, destination lodging (summer season only), and the upper-class clientele were the predominant characteristics until the post-World War II era.

In mid-twentieth century, developers and tourists descend on the landscape and scar the recovering mountainsides with traffic-clogged roads, densely packed houses and condominiums, garish commercial buildings, and scenic vista-blocking high-rise casinos. Cloudy silt-laden streams, smothered meadows, degraded air quality, and decreasing water clarity are the grim costs of urbanization. Environmental groups and long-time residents rise to oppose the actions of development interests.

The decades of the 1970s, '80s, and '90s saw conflict and stalemate play out in courtrooms and public meetings among opposing interests. On the eve of the twenty-first century, a turnaround occurred. The warring parties entered a fragile alliance aimed at reversing the damage. Visualize the rollback and replacement of development, restoration of natural features, and a gradual improvement in the lake's health. These interlocked events and actions made up the ongoing saga of conflicts in Lake Tahoe's human and environmental histories.

In its recorded history, we divide Tahoe into nine notable and often overlapping eras. In each period, the people and their relationship with the environment defined that era's unique characteristics. These eras tend to follow the sequential history of the West's settlement and American progress in general.

Figure 1 shows the eras and their overarching themes in a graphic timeline format. We explain and interpret significant trends and events within these eras to draw the connection between humans' actions and the resulting impact on Tahoe. The numbers on the Figure 2 map enclosed in square brackets on this figure signify where bracketed corresponding general locations of historical points of interest appear in the text.

In describing a historic site, locale, or route, we use the most current geographic or identifying name. We do not devote space to relate an earlier name unless it is historically relevant.

We chose to cite specific examples that are both representative and still visible, allowing the reader to view these notable sites. As such, they may appear inconsistent among each other but are nonetheless correct, given the set of assumptions that is their basis.

Finally, this is an explanatory and interpretive history. We meld the lines of human and environmental accounts, deciding what is relevant and significant to the subject, and apply logical interpretation to place the information in a proper and objective context.

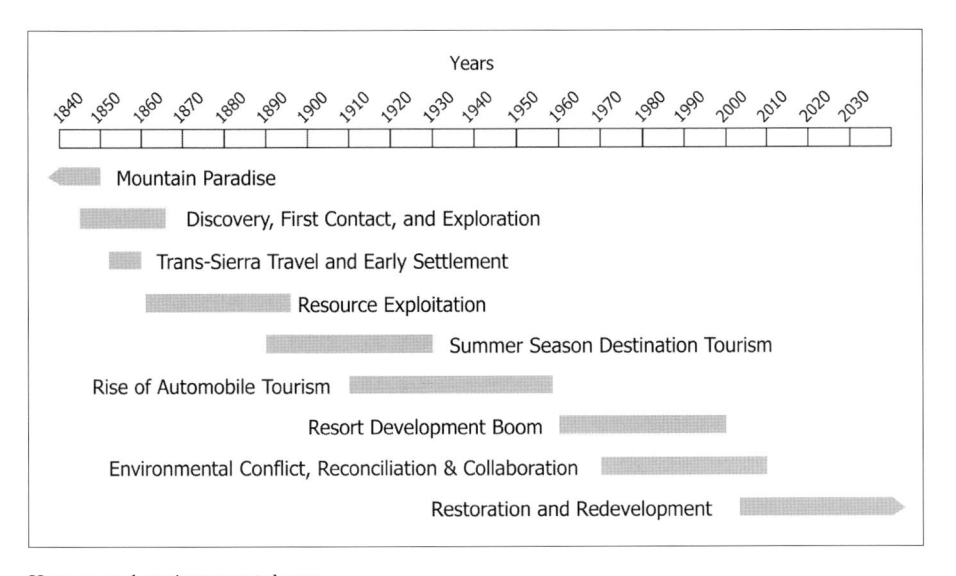

Human and environmental eras.

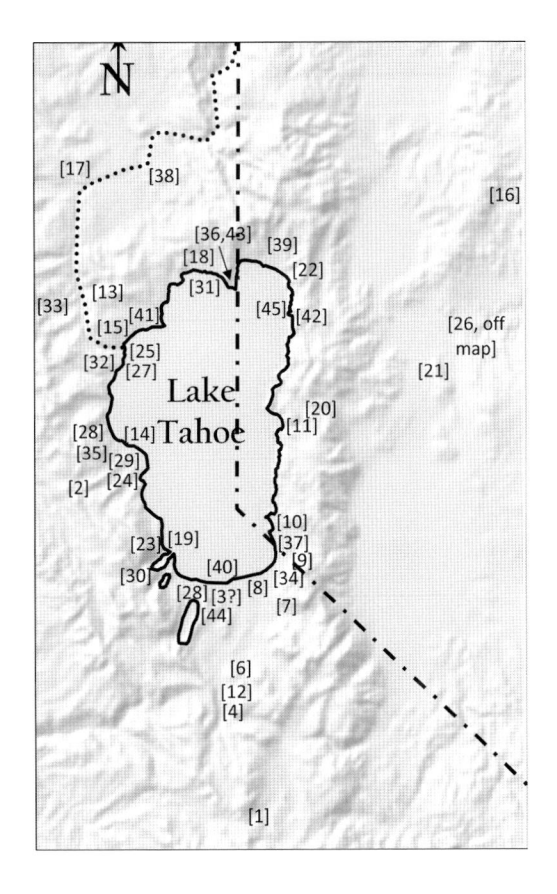

General location map for historical
points of interest.

2

MOUNTAIN PARADISE
(9,000 BCE–1848 CE)

The mountain paradise era was the idyllic summer world of the Washoe tribe at Lake Tahoe before widespread Euro-American invasion of their ancestral lands. It featured native people living in harmony with their environment, leaving nothing but a fleeting ecological imprint on the natural landscape.

We use the Common Era date conventions of BCE (Before Common Era) and CE (Comment Era). The designation BCE following a numbered year indicates "before Year 1," and the designation CE following a numbered year denotes "after Year 1." No designation after a numbered year implies CE.

Anthropological research and archeological evidence inform our current understanding of Native American peoples. Their ancestors crossed an intermittent land bridge from Asia to North America as land became exposed at the conclusion of the last ice age. Some 13,000 years ago, they steadily settled southward over the continent in a natural progression of encampments. Ongoing archeological research and new findings continually refine and revise this scenario of migration and the progression of settlement.

These earliest peoples' descendants inhabited the far western Great Basin and central-eastern Sierra Nevada Mountains for the last 8,000–9,000 years. The last of these successors, the Washoe People, occupied the region and the Tahoe Basin over the previous 1,300 years ending in 1900, an approximate date at which the tribe consistently ceased to live independently and within its traditional cultural norms. Although no reliable population count exists, the region may have supported several thousand tribal members.

The Lake Tahoe Basin was the geographical and spiritual center of the Washoe world. The tribe organized itself into three regional groups that converged at Tahoe during the warmer months. Here they encamped and gathered food to sustain them throughout the barren winter. Tribal members would travel from their wintering grounds in the lower valleys north, east, and south of Lake Tahoe over such main routes as Little Valley-Tunnel Creek, Luther Pass, and other canyons of the Carson Range, gathering at ancestral campsites.

A Washoe family summer encampment at Lake Tahoe. At the time of this photo in 1866, some Washoe had already adopted Western clothing and abandoned their traditional dress of natural plant fibers and animal skins. (*Library of Congress*)

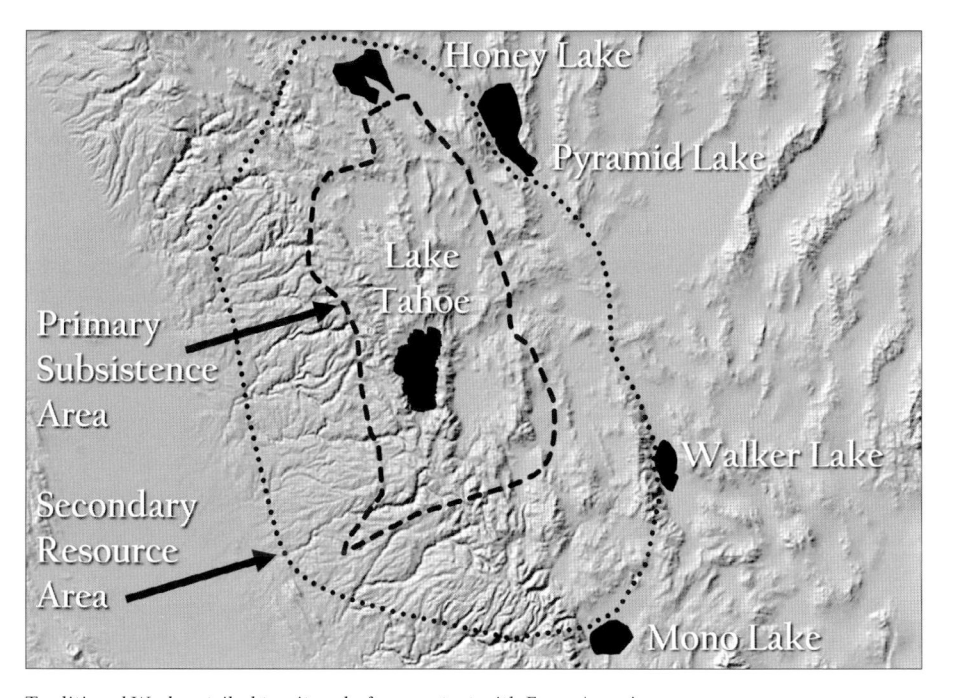

Traditional Washoe tribal territory before contact with Euro-Americans.

Washoe women *c.* 1936 making a rabbit skin quilt with the traditional dome-shaped summer shelters behind them. (*Wikimedia Commons*)

These campsites were on the shoreline near the outlets of unusually productive streams and meadows. The South Shore had an exceptionally high concentration of encampments because of its rich fishery and vast meadow expanse.

Extended families or clans occupied the seasonal encampments. Each camp group selected its leaders who would oversee food gathering and camp life while respecting the other groups' territory. In some cases, tribal men held claim to preferred sites that they passed down through familial generations.

They lived in summer shelters constructed of willows, brush, tree limbs, and animal skins. They made the more durable huts from bark slabs leaning inward against each other, forming a conical-shaped abode.

Fishing and gathering plants were the primary summer activities. Men speared, netted, and trapped whitefish and cutthroat trout, followed by preparation for seasonal storage. The women and children gathered edible plants such as wild raspberries, strawberries and rhubarb, tiger lily, and sunflower seeds. Men hunted mountain sheep, deer, and waterfowl and trapped small mammals and upland game birds.

The Washoe tribe rigorously followed a natural lifestyle. They engaged in primitive agricultural and conservation practices that increased food sources' quality, amount, and reliability. Standard methods were planting, pruning, culling, weeding, rotation, soil loosening, and burning in meadows. Removal of competitor fish species such as Tahoe suckers improved the spawn's success of more desirable species. They followed the conservation principles of taking only males and leaving enough of a species' population to ensure regeneration.

Washoe did not burn the forest, as some may assert. Instead, lightning did this work for them. In any event, the pre-Euro-American contact forest evolved into groves of about 10 acres separated by sparse vegetation as an adaptation to naturally occurring fire. It would have been a significant project for Washoe to ignite a large area of forest. In the end, forest burning had no direct benefit to the tribe and was not worth time and energy for a tribe that often lived on the edge of famine, depending on the whims of nature. They did burn meadows to improve growing conditions and ignited brush fires to drive small mammals into nets.

Washoe women were superb basket weavers. Using willow strands, they wove watertight baskets suitable for cooking using heated rocks submerged into the basket contents. Washoe people used bows and arrows to hunt game and fashioned snowshoes to traverse snow in the winter.

The Washoe culture included a profound spiritual existence that blended the features, phenomena, and symbols of the natural world with the supernatural to explain the tribe's heritage and govern its members' conduct. Shamans imbued with special powers interacted with the mystical world and interpreted natural phenomena to the tribe.

Lake Tahoe was the Washoe tribe's spiritual centerpiece because of its abundance and sacred values. It sustained not only their physical being but also their spiritual existence. In the Washoe's spiritual beliefs, Lake Tahoe's waters imparted life force to all living things. Cave Rock, a prominent geological feature on the East Shore, is a sacred Washoe site.

Washoe basket weaver Dat So La Lee (Louisa Keyser). (*National Park Service*)

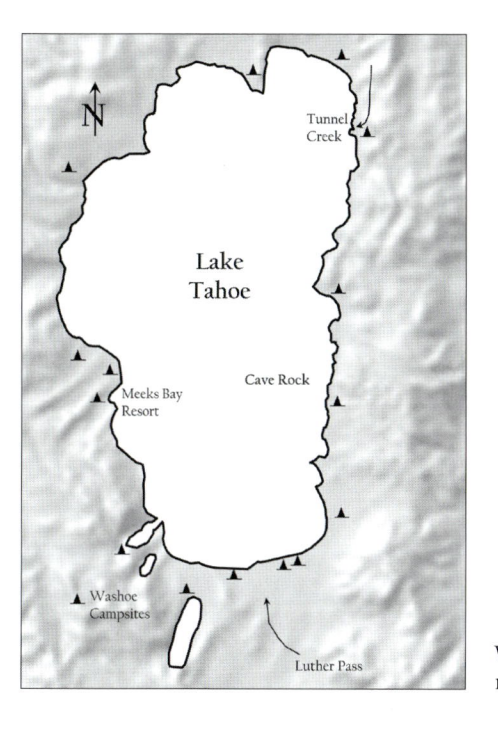

Washoe tribal campsites and some travel routes into the Lake Tahoe Basin.

Hand-tinted postcard image of a Washoe campsite in Emerald Bay. (*Public Domain*)

1875 image of Cave Rock from a
stereoscopic photo. (*Carleton Watkins*)

Before the onset of cold and snow, Washoe people migrated back to their lower elevation wintering grounds where they lived in the more durable structures made of wood bark and small trees. They gathered pine nuts in the fall from pinion pine forests in the lower valleys as a supplemental food source during this period and continued hunting practices there.

In the wake of the 1849 Gold Rush, Euro-American mining and agricultural activities and settlements encroached on native tribes on the Sierra Nevada mountain range's western slope, displacing them. These displacements triggered incursions of these tribes into Washoe territory at Lake Tahoe. This dislocation could spark fierce clashes between tribes. Though the Washoe were a peaceful tribe, Euro-American invaders often settled early conflicts with violence inflicted upon them.

As Euro-American settlement progressed in their home region, settlers forced the Washoe to give up their homelands and traditional life. The tribe had dwindled to 800 by 1864. This alarming decline led the government to conclude in 1866 that the tribe was not likely to survive much longer. Not until 1887 did the tribe receive only small fragments of their ancestral territory in the Carson Valley and Pine Nut mountain range in Nevada, but nothing in its most critical region—the Tahoe Basin. Despite this, the old ways died hard. The migration tradition continued into the early twentieth century, with a few families summering at Tahoe and living on available land. Gradually, Washoe people adapted to western ways finding employment as guides, ranch hands, and laborers. In 1936, the tribe finally gained federal recognition.

Today, the tribe resides in communities in Western Nevada and eastern Alpine County in California. They staged a long overdue Tahoe comeback in 1998 by assuming control of the historic Meeks Bay Resort and managing nearby ancestral lands. The tribe operates the site under a special use permit from the U.S. Forest Service. Also, the tribe manages sacred land on Tahoe's East Shore under a similar arrangement.

The Washoe phrase for the area known as Lake Tahoe is *Da ow a ga*, which translates to "edge of the lake," a place where the Washoe camped. Federal mapmakers in 1862 acted to rename the lake from its former namesake, Confederate-loving former California governor John Bigler. They mispronounced and misspelled the phrase's first sounds, perhaps thinking the syllables rhymed with "Washoe" (Wa-show) to create the Anglo equivalent of the name, "Tahoe."

One would have to look closely to find any physical trace of the pre-historic Washoe culture still visible at Tahoe today. They left very few or no petroglyphs, pictographs, or stationary sculptures; only scattered artifacts of seasonal campsites and grinding rocks remain. Their faint imprint on the land, deteriorated by the passage of time or eradicated by later Euro-American settlement, leaves only scattered archeological remnants as silent testimony to their existence.

The most sacred site, Cave Rock, still stands, protected by restrictions on access to the rock. Washoe elders try to preserve their heritage through oral history and teachings passed through generations and annual celebrations.

The occupation by the Washoe was without any significant or lasting environmental degradation. Yes, the Washoe did manage and modify their environment using the primitive and naturally reversible techniques mentioned earlier in this chapter. Meeting their basic physiological, safety, belongingness, and spiritual needs occupied the lives of the Washoe. They had little time to engage in activities not related to the survival of the individual or the subsistence and cohesion of the tribe.

The tribe's lack of technology and small numbers limited their ability to impact the environment in ecologically irreversible ways. More importantly, the tribe's methods were in harmony with nature, and their practices modeled a balanced ecological existence. Today, the word "sustainable," meaning there are no harmful long-term or irreversible impacts, is the term that describes best their way of life.

For the tribe, Lake Tahoe was its "commons" where all members shared its benefits of abundance and stewardship responsibility. Tribal culture would not condone self-serving behavior in its hunting and gathering. Indeed, the survival of the individual depended on the continued existence of the tribe. Conversely, the tribe's wellbeing relied upon the individual's collaboration and adherence to tribal philosophy.

History recalls the Washoe tribe as the first of many people to love and respect Tahoe in spirit and deed.

3

DISCOVERY, FIRST CONTACT, AND EXPLORATION (1844–1865)

U.S. Army Topographical Corps of Engineers Brevet Captain John C. Fremont left Missouri in June 1843, leading a second topographical expedition to map the Oregon Trail. Fremont was the son-in-law of a prominent U.S. senator and harbored political ambitions. After arriving in the Pacific Northwest in 1843, he left in November of the same year with orders to return to his starting point in Missouri. However, Fremont did not retrace his steps. Instead, he turned southward for an exploratory journey along the Sierra Nevada mountain range's eastern flank in hopes of polishing his image as an explorer.

Fremont sought to discover the legendary Buenaventura River that he believed flowed from the Great Basin to San Francisco Bay. Of course, no such river existed, and others knew it. In midwinter, his party found themselves trapped on the eastern slope of the Sierra Nevada and running low on supplies.

On February 1, 1844, Fremont announced his decision to make a treacherous and challenging crossing of the snowy Sierra Nevada. His destination was Sutter's Fort in the Great Central Valley of California. A Washoe guide recommended against it, characterizing the level of difficulty as "Rock upon rock—rock upon rock—snow upon snow—snow upon snow. Even if you get over the snow, you will not be able to get down from the mountains."

An undaunted Fremont relied on a Washoe Native American guide to point the way to the pass when the desperation of the situation became life-or-death survival. The party adopted the snowshoes used by Washoe tribal members and turned westward into the Sierra Nevada.

On February 14, Fremont's camp was in sight of the pass. He climbed to a high point on Red Lake Peak's western slope (Elev. 10,063 feet) to assess the surrounding terrain [1]. During his observations, he sighted a large lake in the distance. The sighting was not a total surprise. In earlier encounters with local Native Americans, they spoke of a large lake that was the river's source (Truckee River) he had crossed previously. Upon return to camp, he made this journal entry:

> The dividing ridge of the Sierra is in sight from this encampment. With Mr. Preuss [Fremont's surveyor assistant], I ascended to-day the highest peak to the right; from which we had a beautiful view of a mountain lake at our feet, about fifteen miles in length, and so entirely surrounded by mountains that we could not discover an outlet.

Fremont's journal entry became the first recorded sighting of Lake Tahoe by Euro-Americans.

Fremont only had a partial view of the lake. He thus underestimated its actual north–south length of 21 miles because the part visible to him was only 15 miles. He again sighted the lake nine days later as he passed along the Sierra Nevada ridgeline. Here, Fremont could view the eastern extent of the lake previously obscured from his discovery vantage point.

He misunderstood the westward-flowing South Fork of the American River as the lake's outlet from appearance alone. On the expedition record map prepared by Preuss in 1845, the lake appeared too far west and showed a nonexistent southern outlet flowing westward to the Pacific Ocean. Four years later, these errors affected the determination of California's eastern boundary during the statehood boundary discussions.

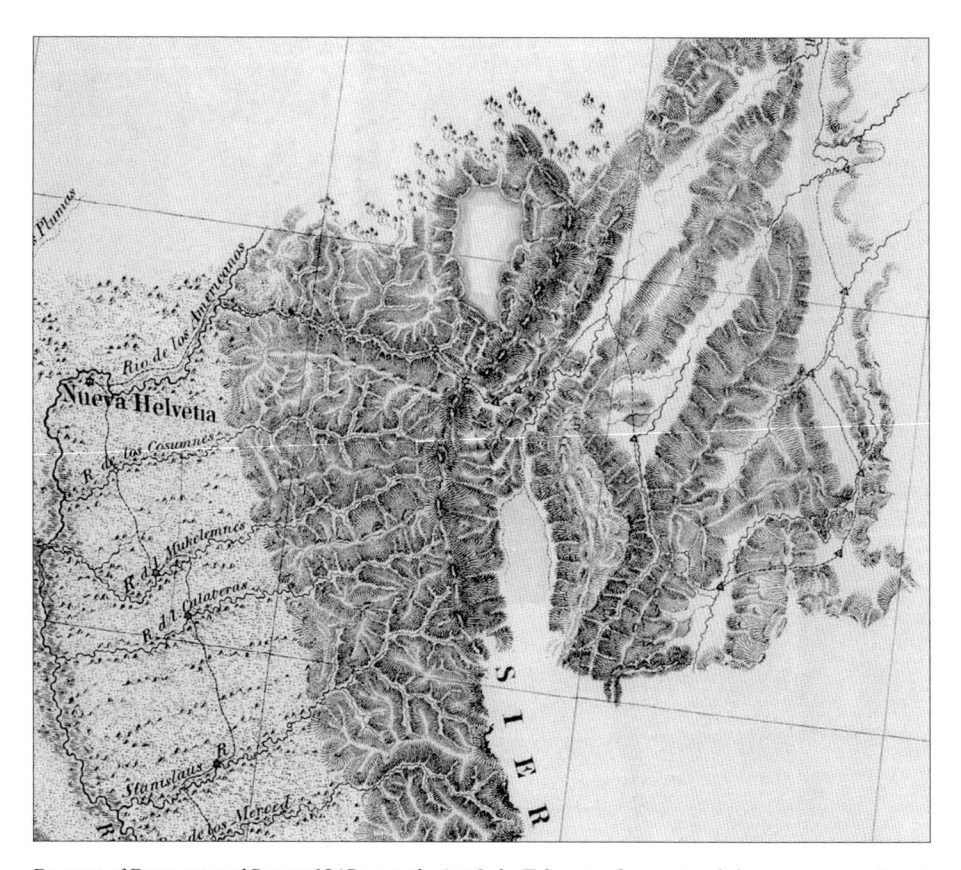

Excerpt of Fremont and Preuss 1845 map placing Lake Tahoe too far west and showing a nonexistent outlet watercourse at its south end. (*Library of Congress*)

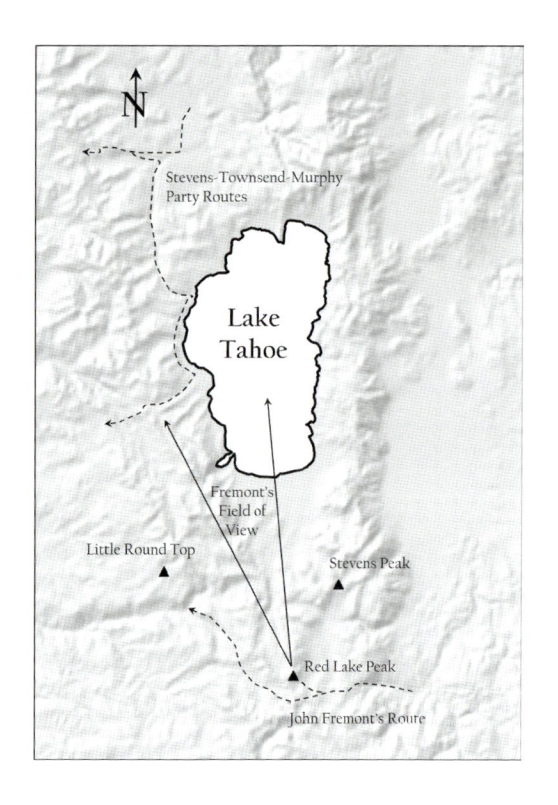

Right: Regional map showing generalized routes for the Stevens, Townsend, and Murphy party and explorer John C. Fremont and Fremont's limited initial Lake Tahoe view.

Below: Lake Tahoe seen from Red Lake Peak [1], the spot of Lake Tahoe's first sighting by Euro-American John C. Fremont. (*Author's collection*)

In Fremont's accompanying report, he christened the water body "Mountain Lake," one of many names that would not last.

There is some ambiguous indication of a possible early visit to Lake Tahoe by a trapping party in late 1844. However, history names the first Euro-American visitors as a splinter group from the first recorded wagon train to cross the Central Sierra Nevada into the Great Central Valley based on sound provenance.

In 1844, the Stevens–Townsend–Murphy Party of fifty-five wagons approached the region using directions given to them in an encounter with a Paiute chief whose indigenous name might have been *Wuna Mucca*. They nicknamed the chief "Truckee" because of his frequent repetition of a similar-sounding Paiute phrase, "tro-kay," which loosely translated means "all right." Using sign language and maps drawn on the ground, he directed them to follow a great river emanating from the Sierra Nevada. They called it the "Truckee River" in his honor.

Arriving exceptionally late in the season near the base of what would later become Donner Pass and with 2 feet of snow already on the ground, their leader, Elisha Stevens, wisely decided to split the party as a survival measure. Again, going by the Paiute's rudimentary directions, six members left camp on horseback on November 15, 1844, while the others followed a westerly heading past an unnamed body of water (Donner Lake) that would take the wagons to the narrow pass they sought. Just missing the onset of the typically snowiest winter months, the horseback group continued along the river's main stem to its source, Lake Tahoe. They continued south along the lake's western shore, followed a well-established Washoe tribal trail west up McKinney Creek, and successfully crossed over Burton's Pass [2] near Miller Lake. Eventually, they reunited with the rest of their party at Sutter's Fort.

Though the Stevens–Townsend–Murphy Party was the precursor of future emigrant crossings of the Sierra Nevada, few Euro-Americans ventured into Tahoe. Emigrants crossing in the region stayed on the most popular and well-established trails and had no defined route to draw them through the Tahoe Basin. A gold-seeker visited briefly in 1850 and was followed a year later by another gold-seeking party. Neither found their illusionary El Dorado but reported back about the extraordinarily scenic high-altitude lake.

Farther back in time in the late 1700s, Spaniards and later Mexicans controlled what would become the southwestern part of the United States, including the Tahoe region. American explorers and emigrants sent back reports describing the region's fabulous resources, encouraging more exploration and settlement. Increasing occupation by American settlers and the manifest-destiny-obsessed United States precipitated the Mexican–American War of 1846–48. The Treaty of Guadalupe Hidalgo forged a peace settlement between the two countries, and the United States paid $15 million for annexed Mexican lands. This new territory covered California, Nevada, Utah, a large part of Arizona, and small areas of Colorado, New Mexico, and Wyoming. Mexico also gave up any claim to the Republic of Texas. Tahoe was now part of the western U.S. territory that directly connected the United States by land to the Pacific Ocean.

In the late 1840s, California was rapidly gaining an immigrant population. The discovery of gold in January 1848 increased overland migration by fiftyfold in 1849 and quickly propelled the unorganized region into statehood by September 1850. After much debate, delegates at the Constitutional Convention of 1849 intended to create a state whose eastern boundary included the Sierra Nevada crest and ran parallel to the Pacific Coast. They selected final borders to parallel the Pacific coastline and capture the Sierra Nevada's watersheds that drained west to the ocean and the Colorado River's west bank. They relied on Fremont's 1845 map as one of their references.

The official map of the state of California of 1850 located most of Lake Tahoe inaccurately outside the state but captured its nonexistent west-flowing southerly outlet as Fremont's map showed. Subsequent surveys would directly position the state's eastern boundary statutory location over Lake Tahoe, cleaving the basin into two spheres of influence, each controlled by one state. This latent condition would erupt a century later into epic struggles between states with remarkably different environmental and land-use policies. Later, four main counties, two in Nevada and two in California, plus two incorporated cities, one in each state, further complicated the two-state situation.

Water rights, population growth, land use, and environmental protection became the political battlegrounds. These conflicts would divide people into two warring camps and eventually entangle the highest levels of state and federal governments.

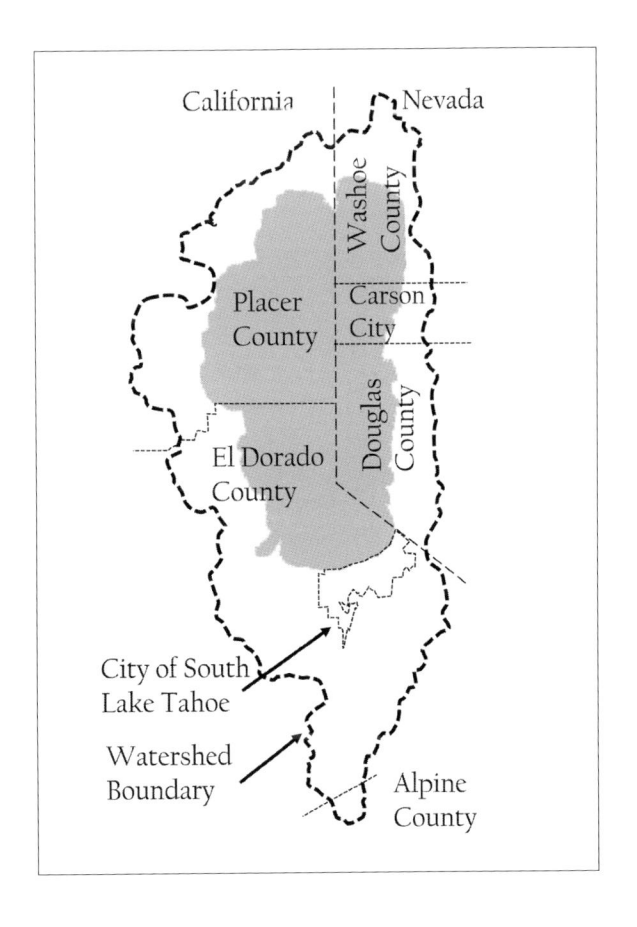

Overlapping governmental agencies.

The 1860–64 survey of California led by State Geologist Josiah Whitney oversaw the earliest scientific report on the Tahoe Basin's natural assets. Its field investigator, Prof. W. H. Brewer, visited Tahoe in 1863. His comparison to European lakes emphasized the absence of any visible human impact at Lake Tahoe. Brewer wrote:

> The purity of its waters, its great depth, its altitude, and the clear sky all combine to give the lake a bright but intensely blue color; it is bluer even than the Mediterranean, and nearly as picturesque as Lake Geneva in Switzerland. Its beautiful waters and the rugged mountains rising around it, spotted with snow which has perhaps lain for centuries, form an enchanting picture. It lacks many of the elements of beauty of the Swiss lakes; it lacks the grassy, green, sloping hills, the white-walled towns, the castles with their stories and histories, and the chalets of the herders—in fact, it lacks all the elements that give their peculiar charm to the Swiss scenery—its beauty is its own, is truly Californian.

No less than Samuel L. Clemens, later to become known as Mark Twain, visited the lake looking to stake a timber claim on its North Shore. He first spied the lake from a high elevation location on the east side near Tunnel Creek in September 1861. He published this unforgettable memory in his 1872 book, *Roughing It*. In it, he recalled the serene and emotionally moving moment, "As it lay there with the shadows of the mountains brilliantly photographed upon its still surface I thought it must surely be the fairest picture the whole earth affords."

Visualizing the increasing popularity of Lake Tahoe in 1865, J. Ross Browne, in his travelogue *Washoe Revisited,* presciently extolled the potential of Tahoe as a resort. He enthusiastically praised its virtues:

> Situated in the bosom of the Sierra Nevada mountains, 6,000 feet above sea level, with an atmosphere of wonderful purity; abounding in game; convenient of access, and possessing all the attractions of retirement from the busy world, amid scenery unrivaled for its romantic beauties, there can be no doubt it will soon become the grand central point of pleasure and recreation for the people of the Pacific Coast.

At that time, the term "Washoe" designated the geographical area encompassing the rich Comstock Lode and western Nevada mining camps.

Both Clemens and Browne saw Tahoe through the lens of its practical usefulness to Euro-Americans, a common philosophy of the time. Preservation for its own sake and future generations would still be many decades away.

While Browne's dreams about the coming tourism economy were visionary, he could not let himself imagine the coming nightmarish plunder of Tahoe's natural assets in the hands of Comstock timber barons, ranchers, water seekers, commercial anglers, and market hunters. At the end of this era, Tahoe remained an unspoiled wilderness mainly unknown to the rest of the world.

4

TRANS-SIERRA TRAVEL AND EARLY SETTLEMENT (1852–1860)

Before 1852, only two wagon routes branched from the California Trail to cross the Central Sierra, bypassing Lake Tahoe. The earlier of the two, the Truckee River–Donner Pass route, pioneered by the Stevens–Townsend–Murphy Party, lay to the north. South of Lake Tahoe was the Carson River Route. A Mexican–American War military unit of the Church of the Latter-day Saints members headed east to Salt Lake City pioneered this route in 1848, approximately following in reverse Fremont's 1844 westward path. Pioneer parties of the late 1840s and early Gold Rush migrants used these routes exclusively and had no reason to detour through Tahoe on their hurried way westward. Old Highway 40 from Truckee to Cisco approximates parts of the Truckee River–Donner Pass route. The Carson Route is known today as part of California Highway 88 and the Mormon Emigrant Trail Road.

Despite the availability of acceptable routes, interest was building in finding more accessible and faster passage over the Sierra Nevada. Travelers came in all forms and modes of transportation. Still, they had one goal in mind—to stake their fortune as quickly as possible in the exploding mining-based economy in California. Many were miners on foot with packs or pushcarts, mounted on horseback, or in wagons with their families; others were merchants, peddlers, and camp followers bent on making their fortune in the secondary economy.

The onslaught of westward travelers attracted by the California Gold Rush became the driving force to develop a faster, more direct route to the goldfields that would accommodate wheeled vehicles. Seizing the opportunity to funnel traffic past his property, rancher and gold miner John "Cockeye" Calhoun Johnson explored a new shortcut through Tahoe and along the canyon of the South Fork of the American River. Johnson's Cutoff was both overall lower in elevation and shorter than either of the other two routes. It had the further advantage of delivering westbound gold-seekers into the heart of California's Mother Lode at Placerville, Johnson's hometown.

At the same time, business interests in the gold rush town of Auburn, Placer County, California, advocated a competing route across Lake Tahoe's North Shore. As it was known, the Placer County Emigrant Road sought to divert travelers from the California Trail near Carson City and over the Carson Range to North Lake Tahoe. At Tahoe, it trended westward parallel to the shoreline and onto the lake outlet. From here, it followed the Truckee River north until the route veered westward again through Olympic Valley, over the crest of the Sierra Nevada, and down the Middle Fork of the American River toward Auburn.

Though promoted as a "road" by Placer County boosters, the route's circuitous nature, rough terrain, lack of roadside services, and narrow width prevented it from attaining popularity. In 1863, it bypassed the difficult Olympic Valley-Middle Fork segment. Instead, it followed the Truckee River from the Tahoe outlet, connecting directly to the Truckee River–Donner Pass route near present-day Truckee. As a trans-Sierra route, it drifted into temporary obscurity. However, in 1859, it received renewed interest as a more direct route to and from the Western Nevada mines, where it became popularly known as the Washoe Trail.

At its beginning in 1852, the wildly successful Johnson's Cutoff was little more than an improved pathway that followed ancient trade routes of Native American tribes. Traveling in a direction toward California, from Carson City, it climbed gradually along Kings Canyon and Clear Creek to Spooner Summit. Turning south, it ascended the Carson Range ridge

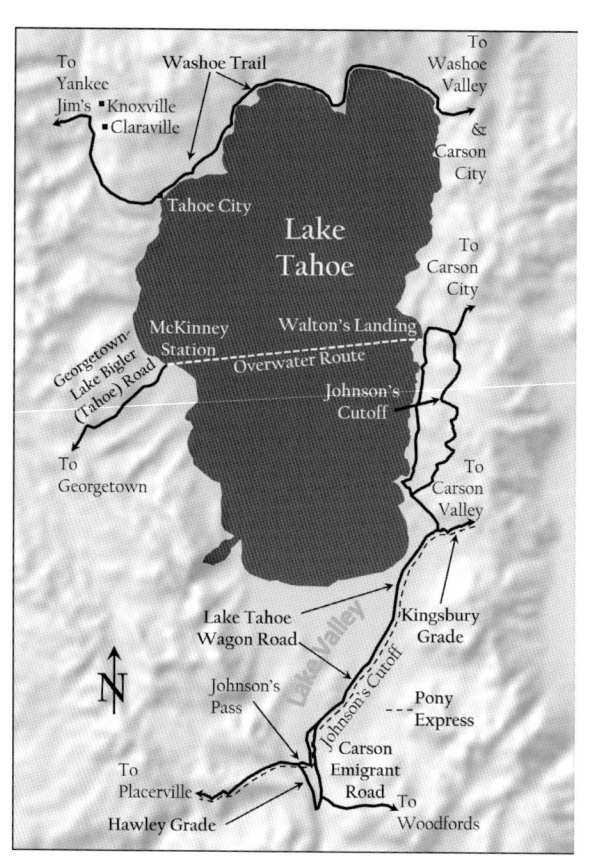

Map of trans-Sierra routes in the Tahoe region.

to parallel the eastern shoreline of Lake Tahoe. After descending to the Lake Tahoe shore near the state line, it swept around the lake's south shore, carefully avoiding soft ground and wide stream crossings by traversing southwest through Lake Valley. Beyond Myers, the road scaled the steep east-facing mountain slope to Johnson's Pass near Lower Echo Lake. The route then descended westward, generally along or parallel to the canyon of the South Fork of the American River and on toward the Sierra Foothills and the heart of California's gold country.

With later improvements, such as a bridge constructed in 1854 over the South Fork of the American River at Riverton, the road became more suitable for wagons. With changes to the route, including a bypass of the Carson Range ridge route, Johnson's Cutoff's destiny was to evolve into the leading nineteenth-century trans-Sierra route—the Lake Tahoe Wagon Road. Today's U.S. Highway 50 corridor from Spooner Summit, and local road Pioneer Trail approximates this historic road's alignment. Its remnants still survive in undisturbed and secluded locations.

In 1852, a bloody skirmish occurred at the south end of the lake [3] due to a reported Native American attack on a pack train headed for Placerville. The Washoe were a peaceful people, and this justification for violence is suspect. In this lopsided clash, 150 Washoe men unsuccessfully fought sixty well-armed "Mountaineer Miners," a volunteer group of mountain men, miners, and Mexican–American War veterans from Placerville. It appears most of the Washoe men were killed, wounded, or escaped, and members of the retaliatory force considered killing the surviving women and children. However, the mountain men in their group wisely persuaded them against it. It would mark a tragic and violent beginning to the disintegration of the traditional Washoe way of life.

As wagon traffic increased to a peak of 350 per day, alternative variations to Johnson's Cutoff route developed further. In 1854, Carson Valley interests promoted a connecting road from the Carson route over Luther Pass that led travelers to Lake Valley's head and a less difficult ascent to Johnson's Pass. Another approach, Kingsbury Grade, began in the Carson Valley near Genoa, Nevada, crossed the Carson Range at Daggett Pass and dropped down to join the main route along the lake's south shore near the state line. With some deviations from the original alignments, both roads continue today as California Highway 89 and Nevada Route 207, respectively.

Some competing routes through Tahoe existed but saw little or no significant traffic, such as the little-used Placer County Emigrant Road. In the 1860s and perhaps earlier, the Georgetown–Lake Bigler (Tahoe) Road received barge traffic at McKinney's from Walton's Landing in Glenbrook. It offered a direct, albeit rugged route for pack trains, to Georgetown, a vital gold mining town set precariously on the dividing ridge between the South and Middle Forks of the American River.

In 1858, El Dorado County contracted with Asa Hawley to build an actual road that lessened the steep ascent to Johnson's Pass and reduced by 5 miles the connecting route over Luther Pass. This well-built road, known today as Hawley Grade, still exists as a popular hiking trail. In 1861, the road gently descended into Lake Valley, ending the need to negotiate the steep incline from Johnson's Pass to the valley floor. In 1863, another major

Freight wagons on the road headed to Tahoe and Northern Nevada mining region. The lead wagon shown here is called a Washoe wagon because it delivers large loads of supplies to the Washoe mining region in Northern Nevada. (*Library of Congress Public Domain*)

realignment occurred with the King's Canyon Toll Road that opened a better route from Carson City to Spooner Summit. Throughout most of its length, gatekeepers extracted tolls for personal income and support for road maintenance and improvements.

Following the silver and gold strikes at the Comstock in the far western extent of the Utah Territory, the Lake Tahoe Wagon Road had become a preferred passage over the Sierra Nevada. It was now serving heavy eastbound traffic into the newly formed Nevada Territory. In 1865, a viaduct for the Lake Tahoe Wagon Road was constructed around Cave Rock, ending the steep climb and descent over the volcanic outcrop. Remnants of the viaduct are still visible today, as is the wagon road segment it replaced. The heavy roadway traffic created demands for lodging, animal fodder, and provisions. It stimulated early settlement of the area along the roadway—the first time a transportation corridor would play a pivotal role in deciding the course of development at the lake.

The first roadhouse appeared in 1851, before the opening of Johnson's Cutoff and suggesting the route may have been in use for individuals on horseback or pack trains. Martin Smith constructed his Lake Valley House, a rudimentary log structure at Lake Valley's head [4] near the strategic junction of Johnson's Cutoff and the Luther Pass trail from the Carson River canyon. He supplied westward-bound travelers with provisions and stock fodder before the pitched climb to Johnson's Pass. Asa Hawley soon joined him with a nearby roadhouse constructed in 1854.

As road traffic increased, more roadhouses appeared at various intervals along the route. These rest stops included Yank's Station (Myers) [6], Sierra House (between Myers and Stateline) [7], Lake House (on the shoreline near the mouth of the Trout Creek) [8], Friday's Station (Stateline) [9], Zephyr Cove House [10], and Glenbrook [11]. These later enterprises offered meals, lodging, provisions, and stock services.

The first stagecoach rumbled over the Sierra Nevada and through the Tahoe Basin in 1857. Butterfield & Company, controlled by Wells Fargo, and Pioneer Stage Company ran rival lines through Tahoe. Pioneer Stage Company connected Placerville, California, and Virginia City, Nevada, with stops at Yank's, Lake House, and Glenbrook. In good conditions, it was possible to make the journey from Carson Valley to Placerville in about twenty-seven hours, including stopovers at waystations. Service continued, subject to road and weather conditions until the Central Pacific Railroad's progress began to capture the trans-Sierra passenger market in 1867.

The short-lived but legendary Pony Express rerouted through Lake Tahoe just after its start in 1860. In about ten days' travel time, the Pony Express carried mail by horse and rider over the 1,966 miles between St. Joseph, Missouri, and Sacramento, California. Horses and riders exchanged with each other at stations along the route. At Tahoe, Friday's Station [9] near Stateline and Yank's Station [6] in Myers were transferring points. In the Tahoe region, westward-bound riders followed the Carson Pass emigrant route south through the Carson Valley, then turned west to enter Tahoe over Kingsbury Grade. They followed this road to its junction with the Lake Tahoe Wagon Road near Stateline and continued

Lake House [8]. (*Library of Congress Public Domain*)

Friday's Station [9]. (*Library of Congress Public Domain*)

along this route to Placerville. The Pony Express service ended October 24, 1861, three days after completing the transcontinental telegraph that ironically followed the same route through Tahoe. The original Friday's Station building still stands on the northeast corner of Lake Parkway and U.S. Highway 50 in Nevada.

Trans-Sierra travel continued throughout the mid-nineteenth century as commerce moved back and forth across a county that now spanned a continent from the Atlantic Ocean to the Pacific Ocean. Wagon traffic was heavy as California became the supply center for Western Nevada's mines until the Central Pacific and Virginia & Truckee railroads started in 1869.

Ranches and farms sprang up around the lake to supply replacement stock, vegetables, meat, dairy products, and hay. The vast expanse of meadows surrounding the lake yielded cut grass and supported grazing. In some cases, shipping on the lake transported agricultural products, initially by sailing ships and later by steamers. The sailing vessel *Iron Duke* was the first sizable ship on Tahoe's waters and hauled hay and provisions. Local agriculture later supplied the early seasonal resorts but declined due to competition from the Sacramento Region.

A significant agricultural enterprise was the Celio Ranch [12], founded in 1863 in Lake Valley. The ranch produced both dairy products and beef cattle. Livestock was driven in the spring to Tahoe from the lower elevation winter ranch in the Sierra Foothills. During the summer, cattle grazed on high meadows. In later years, the ranch operations included milled lumber production and tourist services.

A highly speculative silver mining boom supplied the seeds of the first settlements in the northern part of the lake and the primitive beginnings of the tourism industry. A stampede

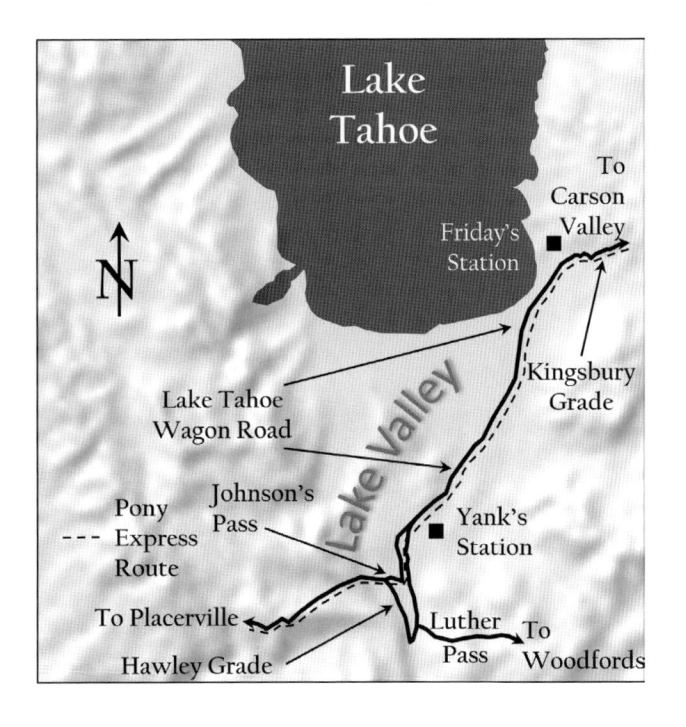

Pony Express route through Tahoe.

of miners from Mother Lode towns and Georgetown arrived at two short-lived mining camps. The mining camps of Knoxville [13] and nearby Claraville were along the Truckee River, about 6 miles downstream from the Lake Tahoe outlet and near the mouth of Olympic Valley. The mining boom collapsed as quickly as it started and was all but finished in 1864.

A few disappointed miners made the best of a bad situation. Perhaps sensing changes were underway at Tahoe, they settled along the north and west shores to pursue more productive occupations. Some became anglers, others followed an agrarian path, and still, others constructed establishments to serve local loggers and some of the first visitors coming for pleasure. Many of their surnames would eventually provide names for prominent topographic features—Blackwood Creek, McKinney Creek, Ward Valley, Madden Creek, and Barker Pass.

On the western shore, John McKinney constructed a hunting lodge and pier [14] that later became a popular resort hotel, Chamber's Landing, with an overwater bar. Another miner, a French-German immigrant named William Pomin (originally, Pomine), would become the founder of the first town at the lake, Tahoe, later known as Tahoe City [15].

Modern-day Tahoe City traces its roots to 1863–4 when Pomin and others laid out a townsite including a lakefront common. In 1864, Pomin constructed a house of sawed lumber for his family. That same year saw the construction of a crib pier on the lakefront and a small hotel. Pomin opened a competing enterprise in 1868 that he named Tahoe House and later joined by his brothers. In 1869, others built a hotel that eventually became the eighty-four-room Grand Central Hotel in 1873.

Tahoe City in 1873 [15]. (*North Lake Tahoe Historical Society*)

Remarkably, direct descendants of the Pomins still live in the area. The Pomins and descendants of the Celio family of Lake Valley are among the families with the most pro-longed continuous residence in the Tahoe Basin. Today, Tahoe City still has its small-town ambiance. Slower growth, distance from Nevada casinos, and strict environmental regu-lations spared it from the engulfing wave of land development and gaming that eventually smothered Tahoe's south end.

Several large-scale western surveys—including Henry de Groot (1859), W. H. Brewer (1863), and G. M. Wheeler (1871)—covered the Lake Tahoe region. However, in 1861, the federal gov-ernment did the first detailed survey to set up the Nevada Territory. It was not until 1865 that surveyors mapped the California side, though California had achieved statehood in 1850. The 1861 Nevada Territory survey delineated albeit inaccurate California State–Nevada Territorial Line, placing much more of Lake Tahoe in California than previously thought in 1850.

At the close of this era, Tahoe was still an unspoiled wilderness with a few settlements composed of seasonal hotels, summer encampments, roadhouses, farms, ranches, and small lumbering operations scattered around the lake. The Washoe tribe had been driven out and replaced by low-intensity agriculture. A few people had begun to visit Tahoe for pleasure and health. Elsewhere, the blast of deep-shaft mining and the roar of the railroad locomotive would signal impending environmental change. It would be the last time Tahoe would rest undisturbed, sheltered from nineteenth-century western civilization's detrimental effects.

To rewrite with a twist Mark Twain's legendary quote upon seeing Lake Tahoe for the first time—as it lay there peaceful and undisturbed, I could not have thought it would become one of the fiercest pictures of environmental conflict the whole Earth affords.

5

RESOURCE EXPLOITATION
(1861–1896)

In the 1860s, two significant developments during western settlement would create conditions ripe for resource exploitation and eventually inflict environmental changes at Tahoe that still reverberate. In 1859, the Comstock Lode discovery and the Big Bonanza in 1873 revealed vast silver and gold ore lodes around Virginia City, Nevada [16]. Construction of the transcontinental railway began in 1863 with an alignment [17] that passed just north of Lake Tahoe. These events would converge to seal the fate of the Tahoe Basin's natural endowments—its forests, scenic vistas, water resources, and natural habitat—and its aboriginal residents.

Responding to the influx of population because of the precious metals strike and as a precursor to statehood, Congress authorized the Nevada Territory organization in 1861. They implemented this action by cutting the newly formed territory away from the expansive Utah Territory covering the Great Basin's central section. The legislated western boundary of the Nevada Territory initially overlapped with California but would later be coterminous with California's existing eastern boundary. This divided Lake Tahoe, placing the east extent of the Tahoe Basin within the new territorial government's authority and setting the stage for years of disputes over its future. The Nevada Territory eventually achieved statehood on October 31, 1864.

In 1860, aggressive deep shaft silver mining began on the Comstock Lode. The combination of depth, the width of the veins, and unstable soil conditions required the intensive use of wood shoring to prevent the collapse of subsurface excavations. Inspired by the combs in beehives, mining engineer Philip Deidesheimer invented the "square set" mine-shoring technique to deal with these complex challenges. Square set mineshaft shoring used 16-inch square wood timbers, 7 feet long, to construct cubical cribs filled with waste rock to support the excavation in all directions.

On the ground surface that overlaid the mines, housing, commercial buildings, and industrial structures created the demand for sawed lumber. Cordwood supplied the need for heating and fuel. By 1876, Virginia City mines and the settlement itself consumed

Partial view of Virginia City in 1875 [16]. (*Carleton Watkins, Wikimedia Commons*)

80 million board feet of lumber and 250,000 cords of fuel word annually, most of it from the Tahoe Basin.

With the insatiable demand for wood products, mills appeared and began producing from stands on the Carson Range's east slope. By 1861, the demand outstripped production capability, and the most accessible woodlands were nearing exhaustion. In response, lumbering companies reached out to grasp new stands of timber. The vast forest at Tahoe, with its proximity to future rail lines, was a logical source. Ponderosa, Jeffrey, and sugar pines were the preferred species because of their structural integrity. Forested land covered 94,740 acres or about 47 per cent of the tributary watershed.

On the heels of the silver boom, the Central Pacific Railroad had become a significant direct and indirect influence on regional lumber demand. The railroad itself needed structural lumber, such as the 300 million board feet of sawed lumber needed to construct 40 miles of snowsheds over the Sierra summit. A board foot of lumber is a volume of wood 1 foot wide, 1 foot long, and 1 inch thick. At one point, Central Pacific locomotives consumed 75,000 cords of Tahoe fuelwood in one year. A cord is a stack of split wood 4 feet high, 4 feet deep, and 8 feet long. The construction of railroad tracks, bridges and buildings, and new towns' development commanded prodigious lumber quantities along the newly laid rail line.

Massively large trees—up to 3 feet in diameter on the East Shore and up to 5 feet on the North and West Shores—populated the forest. The oldest trees were 200–300 years old. The pre-logging Tahoe forest was a mature and diverse mixed-conifer forest with about 55 percent falling into the category of old growth and the balance in various late maturity stages. Trees grew in isolated groves of about 10 acres, separated by light-density vegetation. Predominant forest species were the Jeffrey pine, ponderosa pine, and sugar pine. Incense cedar, lodgepole, white fir, and red fir species filled out the forest diversity. Trees were well spaced with about 45 percent tree cover and 900 trees per acre. Due to shading by the dense canopy, the understory was a sparse 20 percent of groundcover.

Lightning caused wildfires were a health-restoring process, burning out the dense undergrowth of brush and smaller trees and limited in scale. These fires burned through at twenty to thirty-year intervals scorching the equivalent of 30 acres per day. These kept understory and sapling growth down but did minor damage to the more mature trees. The forest's natural growth pattern in discrete groves separated by wide belts of thin vegetation proved to be an effective deterrent to widespread wildfires.

Government explorer Captain James H. Simpson visited the area in 1859 and found, "The pines of various kinds are very large, and attain a height of probably from 100 to 150 feet. Their diameter is not infrequently as much as 8 feet, and they sometimes attain the dimension of 10 feet." An early observer noted the forests of Tahoe were "... dominated by giant pine trees with so much room on the forest floor that riders could travel at full gallop without losing their hats." Logging company owner Duane L. Bliss estimated most of the trees he cut were 150–350 years old.

In September 1861, Samuel L. Clemens (a.k.a. Mark Twain) trekked up from Carson City to Lake Tahoe to stake a speculative timber claim in present-day Tahoe Vista. He later wrote that the trees on his claim were "one to five feet at the butt."

Pre-contact forest, c. 1886. View of Emerald Bay and Rubicon Point [19]. (*University of Nevada Special Collections*)

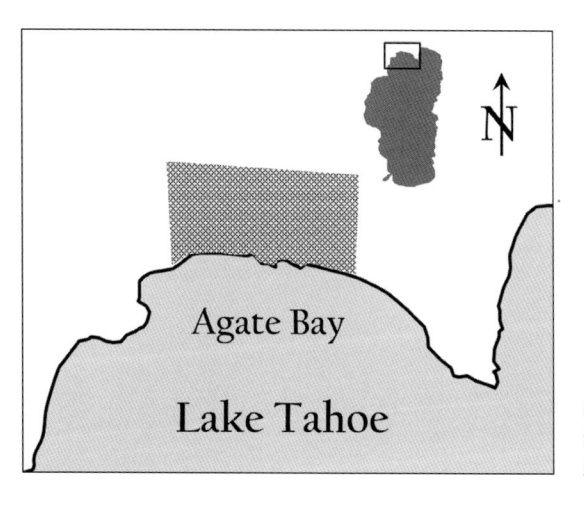

Samuel Clemens' (Mark Twain) timber claim location [18]. (*Fairest Picture—Mark Twain at Lake Tahoe*)

Clemens intended to homestead land in the newly created Nevada Territory. Instead, he futilely carved out his claim on Agate Bay's shore [18] within the boundaries of California. He camped at Stateline Point [19]. Inaccurate mapping, conflicting statutory state and territorial boundaries, and unfamiliarity with the terrain caused his error. Added to this misstep and through his inattentiveness, his campfire ignited a wildfire that damaged his would-be "timber ranch." Despite these setbacks, he nonetheless kept an indelibly vivid impression of the area's natural beauty that eventually seeped into his lectures, essays, and books and firmly cemented Lake Tahoe's uniqueness in American lore. Like many who visited after him, the Tahoe Conflict confronted him. He came to Tahoe to exploit but left with a deep spiritual connection and a humbling reverence for this special place.

At least four sawmills were in operation at Tahoe in 1861, initially serving settlement needs. The largest was the Lake Bigler Lumber Company of Glenbrook [11], controlling 1,000 acres of nearby lands. By 1863, the company was hauling finished lumber by wagon over the Carson Range to Virginia City.

Coincident with the Big Bonanza's discovery in 1873, the Carson & Tahoe Lumber & Fluming Company (CTLF), a farsighted partnership led by principals Duane L. Bliss and Henry M. Yerington with low-profile financial backer D. O. Mills, acquired the Lake Bigler Lumber Company assets. They promptly made improvements to ramp up production significantly for the Comstock. CTLF added a second lakefront mill to receive rafted logs from around the lake and constructed 8.75 miles of a narrow-gauge rail line to haul finished lumber 900 feet in elevation from lake level at Glenbrook to 7,200 feet at Spooner Summit [20]. It acquired and improved 11 miles of an existing waterborne flume to economically float its wood products from Spooner Summit to Carson City [21]. The flume was fed water from Marlette Lake and Spooner Lake reservoirs and side streams along the flume's route.

From Carson City, the Yerington controlled Virginia & Truckee Railroad transported CTLF lumber products at preferred rates to its primary market in Virginia City. At peak production, the CTLF could produce 150,000 board feet of lumber per day from two sawmills.

Glenbrook sawmill complex, *c*. 1888 [11]. (*University of Nevada Special Collections*)

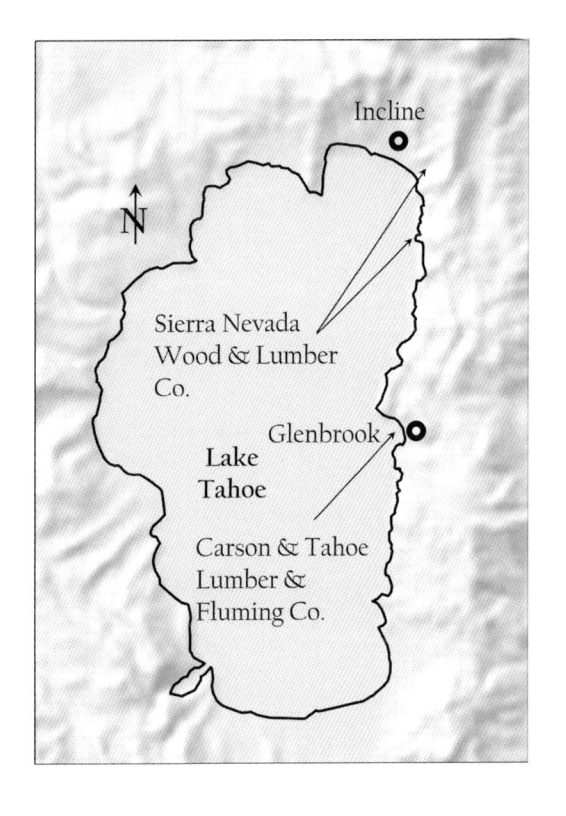

Map of two sawmill complexes on the East Shore.

As the major lumber producer in the Tahoe Basin, CTLF, during its twenty-three-year heyday, produced 750 million board feet of lumber and 500,000 cords of wood from 17,500 acres owned, and another 30,000 acres leased to supply cut logs by contract loggers. It was not until the middle of the twentieth century that the company disposed of its most extensive landholdings and entered corporate dissolution.

The complementary partnership of lumberman Walter S. Hobart and engineer Samuel H. Marlette founded another significant lumber producer, the Sierra Nevada Wood & Lumber Company (SNWL), in 1879. SNWL built its mill and finished lumber transport facilities near present-day Incline Village, Nevada [22].

If the Bliss, Yerington, and Mills production facilities were massive, the much smaller Hobart and Marlette physical works were spectacular. Logs rafted across the lake to Sand Harbor or extracted from nearby forests were loaded onto railcars that rolled on 6 miles of rail lines along the lakeshore, converging at the mill site. Workers loaded cut lumber onto a 4,000-foot-long cable-drawn incline railway to a waterborne flume 1,400 feet above the mill. In a cooperative venture with the Virginia City & Gold Hill Water Company, lumber was then flumed 1.5 miles south. It entered the water company's 4,000-foot tunnel, easterly through the Carson Range, where it emerged above the Washoe Valley for its second ride on 9 miles of a flume to the Virginia & Truckee Railroad spur in the Washoe Valley.

From Washoe Valley, the bulk of SNWL production moved north by rail to the Central Pacific mainline in Reno for distribution to distant markets. The rest was transported east by rail on the Virginia & Truckee to Virginia City for use as mine shoring, construction lumber, and fuelwood.

Two aqueducts converging on the inlet of the tunnel fed the flume transport system. Six major streams fed the north aqueduct in the northeast quadrant of the basin. It continued its southward journey picking up finished lumber as it passed the top of the SNWL incline railway toward its terminus at the tunnel inlet. The south aqueduct carried water stored in Marlette Lake to the tunnel inlet, where it joined with the north aqueduct to create the combined flow through the tunnel. These aqueducts formed the production arteries of the historic Virginia City and Gold Hill water system. During its seventeen years of operation, SNWL produced 200 million board feet of lumber and 1 million cords of wood from 55,000 acres of forest lands. As the Comstock demand slackened, the company sold its remaining Tahoe holdings to CTLF in 1894, dismantled its Tahoe mill, and moved its center of operations to Hobart Mills, 7 miles north of Truckee, California. Eventually, it would grow into the largest lumber producer in the Tahoe-Truckee region.

Local nineteenth-century logging methods were at the same time traditional and unique. Target tree species were hand-sawed at the base and felled or wastefully dropped using a detonation of explosives within the trunk base. Logs were limbed, cut into manageable lengths, and the sharp edge on one end cut away to accommodate later sliding and fluming. Draft animals dragged the log segments along skid trails directly to the lakeshore, if nearby, to log-lined chutes, or where enough water was available, temporary V-flumes made of stout wood boards. Tallow lubricated the sides for the log-lined chutes, and draft animals pulled the logs, or gravity alone propelled them down steep slopes to the loading area.

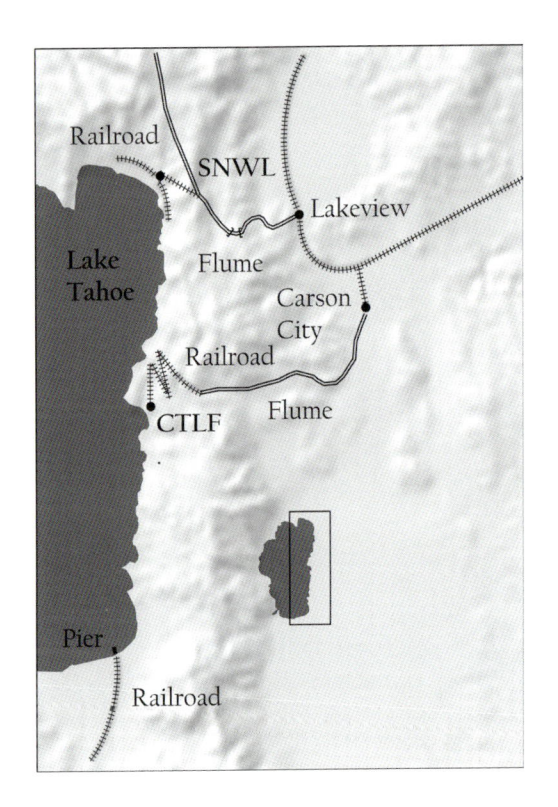

Finished lumber transport
infrastructure to supply Virginia City
and the Central Pacific Railroad.

Cut logs on oxen-drawn wagon intended to be lifted into the water using a tripod. (*LDS Church History Library*)

A boom of logs prepared for towing across the lake to the sawmill. (*University of Nevada Special Collections*)

At the loading area, workers used ramps to load logs onto draft animal-drawn wagons or flatcars on a temporary railway for transport to the beach.

Accumulated logs at the lakeshore were moved into the water using a tripod lift, launched, and gathered into "booms" of floating logs for rafting across the lake to the mills. In 1887, CTLF used a railway to transport logs from Lake Valley to a pier where the cut logs were rolled off flat cars into the water and gathered into booms. SNWL log booms were beached at Sand Harbor and loaded onto its railway leading to the sawmill. CTLF released its log booms into Glenbrook Bay, where they were extracted mechanically from the water and fed directly to two lakefront sawmills.

In a departure from the popular practices of rafting logs to mills on the east side of the lake, the Donner Lumber and Boom Co. cut timber around the Lake Tahoe outlet and the canyon walls of the Truckee River but processed the logs in Truckee. It constructed and operated the first dam, a wooden splash dam of buttress design, at the Lake Tahoe outlet. The company transported its cut logs to the Truckee sawmills in "drives" on the Truckee River floated by surges of floodwater released from its dam.

The towing of log booms required steam-powered watercraft. The first such craft was the Steamer *Governor Blasdell*, constructed by the Lake Bigler Lumber Company. Other steamers were launched and put into towing service, making up a fleet of eight such vessels during the peak logging years. Some steamers also saw service for shipment of freight, passenger transport, and pleasure excursions. Some owners beached their steamers at the end of their useful life and scavenged them; other owners scuttled them in deep water, and some vessels refitted to lead new lives as tour boats for the burgeoning tourism industry.

The primary innovation that made lumber production possible and profitable was the V-flume, a wooden trough with a V-shaped cross-section that floated logs and timber products down to a collection point. Other innovations included leasing timber rights from surrogate land claimants and hiring contractors to supply cut logs. Crews of Chinese loggers scavenged lopped tree limbs, logs unsuitable for structural lumber, and undesirable white fir trees.

Duane L. Bliss may have decreed that no cutting of trees less than 15 inches in diameter should occur. Some have interpreted this as a resource conservation measure. However, if he mandated such a policy, it was presumably to avoid the economic inefficiency of handling logs too small to have any monetary value.

The costly difficulty of moving logs to the lakeshore and the depressed demand spared an area [23] north of Emerald Bay from logging, and CTLF donated the land that became D. L. Bliss State Park. In other cases, loggers left a few mature trees on ridgelines in the belief they would be the source of forest reseeding on the denuded slopes below.

The Tahoe Conflict played out its first act during this era, and the protectionist view of Tahoe lost out by a wide margin. While more than a few persons decried the forest practices of the period, most believed it was a waste to leave forests untouched, viewed it as a resource of inexhaustible proportions, or concluded it was an unavoidable necessity for Euro-American settlement of the West. In 1876, author Dan De Quille made the intelligent and oft-quoted observation, "The Comstock lode [*sic.*] may truthfully be said to be the tomb of forests of the Sierras." After visiting the lake in 1877, a writer quoted in *Scientific American* characterized Tahoe lumbermen as "an industrious gang of vandals" and decried the "curious litter of chips and shavings represents a forest sacrificed."

View of the ridge south of Meeks Bay [24] in the 1930s showing the extent of nineteenth-century tree removal. The trees in the photo were too small to be cut during the logging of the ridge in the 1880s. (*University of Nevada Special Collections*)

In 1880, a congressional public lands committee attempted to investigate CTLF forest practices. Duane L. Bliss described his company's procedure of buying the land from others (who had acted as surrogates to circumvent the statutory individual limit of 160 acres on homestead acreage), cut the merchantable timber, and then abandoned the ground to avoid paying taxes. He added defensively that the company was now scavenging logging slash (wasted limbs and culled logs) rather than leaving it to rot and burn on the forest floor.

In yet another scene in the Tahoe Conflict historical play, the California Legislature created the Lake Bigler (Tahoe) Forestry Commission in 1883 to assess logging companies' activities. However, despite widespread scientific support, the commission met with no success when it proposed creating a California state park. The proposal was the first of many such efforts to preserve the Tahoe Basin. As was common in the era, the government decided the Tahoe Conflict on the side of individual benefit and industrial progress. It is interesting to note that "industrial tourism" was a popular pastime during this era. In this genre, well-to-do visitors traveled to the country's scenes of industrial progress as an act of patriotism and to show worshipful loyalty to American capitalism.

Widespread logging for structural wood products ended in 1896 due to resource depletion and evaporated demand from the collapsed mining boom. In its wake, small-scale local operations arose and continued into the mid-twentieth century. At the south end of the lake, the Celio mill continued to be a significant employer into the late 1940s. Suppliers to a paper mill located downstream on the Truckee River cut white fir and second growth on the lake's north end. Limited localized logging continued for a while in Ward Valley, supplying local needs and feeding the then-dominant sawmill industry in Truckee. In contrast, a small sawmill produced dimension lumber near Tahoe City.

As the lumbering boom closed at the end of the nineteenth century, timber companies had taken two-thirds of the roughly 95,000 acres of Tahoe's forest with most acreage clear-cut. The remaining standing forest and some second growth fell in the early twentieth century, leaving only 3–5 percent of the original forest as small, scattered fragments and lone trees spared due to undesirable species, wrong size, or structural defect. In the Tahoe Conflict's final act over forests, exploitation for the individual and corporate benefit and societal progress won out.

The pattern of private ownership of large tracts was both a burden and a godsend. Since Tahoe lands passed early into private hands for unfettered use, it prevented enlightened late-nineteenth century protection through public ownership. Conversely, in later years, private parties acquired extensive tracts, many of whom kept their holdings intact. Some sold to government buyers eager to consolidate broad land holdings into the new concept of national forests. The large parcels enabled public acquisition for state parklands and transfers into the newly created national forest system during the ensuing conservation movement of the twentieth century.

Major state parks, including Lake Tahoe Nevada State Park, Sand Harbor State Park, Ed Z'berg Sugar Pine Point State Park, D. L. Bliss State Park, Van Sickle Bi-State Park, and Burton Creek State Park, trace their roots to these large landowners. At the end of the nineteenth century, private owners controlled 85 percent of Tahoe lands. Over 100 years

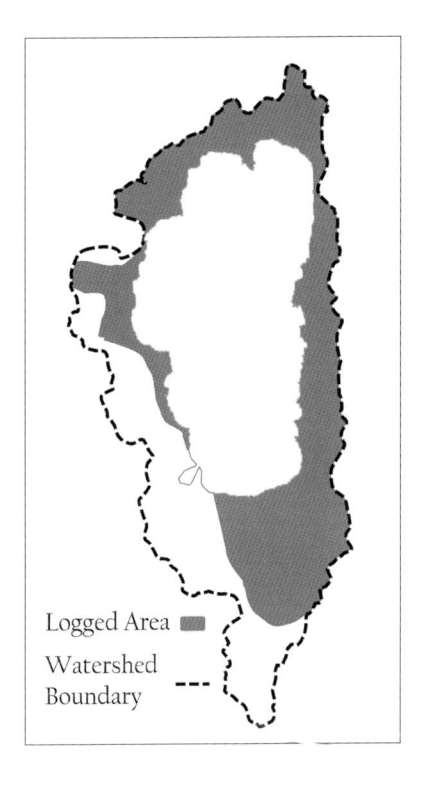

Map showing the logged area in the Tahoe Basin.
(*Adapted from Lake Tahoe Watershed Assessment*)

later, public agencies owned 88 percent of the land and 45.2 percent of the shoreline and intended to increase their holdings.

Lake bottom sediment cores tell a horrific story of massive soil erosion and wood debris deposited into the lake. Runoff carried logging slash and eroded soil from roads, skid trails, and log chutes into the lake. Beaches became choked with logging debris that washed ashore. Sawmills dumped bark, sawdust, and other mill waste directly into the lake or stockpiled it into mounds for open burning. A thick pall of smoke from fuelwood burning for steam power and uncontrolled wildfires on the denuded and logging slash-strewn forest lands fouled the air. Cutover forest and fragmented woodlands led to decreases in animal life. Water quality and lake clarity suffered mightily during this period and its immediate aftermath. However, the lake's natural pollution assimilative capacity, the regeneration of vegetation cover in the watershed, and the abrupt cessation of a significant disturbance in the watershed allowed the lake to recover much of its pristine properties by the middle of the twentieth century.

Today, the forests of Tahoe continue to suffer from their intensive clear-cutting history, drought, and fire suppression. The second-growth forest has recovered with trees too dense and dominated by drought-sensitive tree species, such as white fir, that quickly ascended because of the removal of shading by the overstory and the wet cycles that followed massive tree removal.

A well-intentioned twentieth-century national policy of fire suppression on public lands never allowed the occurrence of health-restoring natural fires that would have thinned and culled the second-growth forest. The result is an unhealthy forest stand where up to 25 percent of standing trees are dead or dying and cause an extreme fire hazard. In a catastrophic wildfire, the resulting burned watershed will exert devastating and long-term impacts on the environment's health and quality of life in the basin. Sadly, this alarming situation was borne out in major wildfires occurring in 2002, 2007, and 2021.

Tahoe fisheries were at one time plentiful and diverse, having sustained many generations of Washoe. However, like its forests, Tahoe fisheries were highly vulnerable to exploitation. Tahoe once held large populations of marketable species of native Lahontan cutthroat trout and mountain whitefish. Commercial fishing commenced in 1859 and intensified beginning in the 1870s as anglers supplied tens of thousands of pounds of fish annually to markets in San Francisco, Virginia City, and cities further distant. The California Legislature banned commercial fishing at Lake Tahoe in 1917, but it was too late. By 1938, the fishery had collapsed because of fishing pressure, water diversions, destruction of spawning habitat, human-caused obstructions to fish passage, and invasive species introduction. More recently, a related strain of the native Lahontan cutthroat has been reintroduced into isolated tributaries such as Cascade Lake and Marlette Lake to rebuild a breeding population and pure strain of these native fish.

Between 1880 and 1971, freshwater biologists tinkered with the lake's aquatic ecology. They sought to build up a sustainable fishery by introducing new species. Brook, rainbow, and brown trout were among the early arrivals by 1900. By 1912, planted lake trout became prevalent. Planting crayfish (1934) and Mysis shrimp (1963) sought to create a sustainable food chain to support the newly introduced species. A final fish introduction occurred accidentally when a holding pond for Kokanee salmon overflowed in 1944, allowing the population to take hold in Lake Tahoe.

The net result of the species introductions coupled with environmental changes was a partial collapse of the aquatic ecosystem and a decline of native species. The extirpation of the native Lahontan cutthroat trout occurred in 1939.

By 1964, the native Lahontan redside shiner and speckled dace were in severe decline. The collapse of the Daphnia population of native aquatic zooplankton followed these alarming developments in the early 1970s.

In the case of fisheries, the Tahoe Conflict has resolved adversely to the aquatic environment. In a well-meaning but grossly uninformed effort to reverse the damage, state agencies introduced non-native fish species to replace those native fishes wiped out by decades of unregulated takings and habitat destruction. In support of the previously introduced species' struggling population, stocking of non-native prey species followed. The result was worse than if they had done nothing in the aftermath of the extirpation (local extinction) of the native Lahontan cutthroat trout species. It vividly illustrates how the ability of humans to change their environment exceeds their ability to foresee and concern themselves with the effects of those changes. Today, such actions are unthinkable and nearly impossible given our increase in scientific knowledge and the gauntlet of permits and studies such proposals must pass before approval.

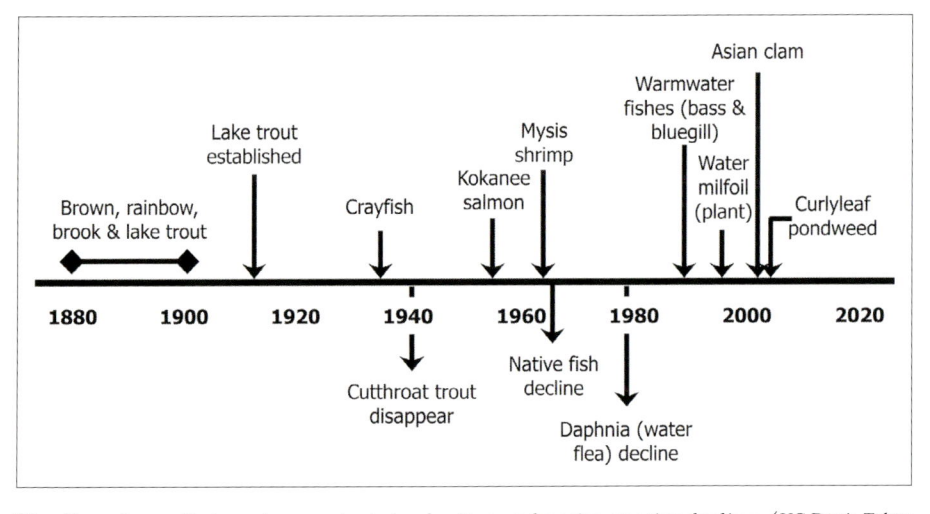

Timeline of aquatic invasive species introduction and native species decline. (*UC Davis Tahoe Environmental Research Center*)

Lahontan cutthroat trout. (*U.S. Fish and Wildlife Service*)

Grazing to produce animal products began in the 1860s initially to supply Nevada mining populations and continued as production shifted to meet local demand from way stations, hotels, and seasonal residents. Sierra foothill and Carson Valley ranches drove thousands of head of cattle and sheep into the basin annually. At their peak, no fewer than thirteen commercial dairies occupied lower elevation meadows. Intensive grazing of sheep continued into the mid-twentieth century and consumed most herbaceous plants and grasses on rangelands. A natural resource specialist visiting the area in 1900 noted that except for the fenced, high meadows grazed by cattle, the lower elevation range was devoid of forage except for a few hardy shrubs and broadleaf trees.

While grazing animals may appear passive and rustic, they extracted a severe toll on the watershed. Intense grazing and trampling by livestock destroyed the last of the plant materials used by the Washoe people, reduced vegetation regeneration, and contaminated surface waters with manure waste. Sheepherders set repetitive, seasonal fires to improve range conditions and suppress non-forage plant regeneration, thus hurting biodiversity. One U.S. Forest Service hydrologist remarked in the 1970s that historically intense grazing correlated to excessive stream channel cutting and erosion observed in the Blackwood Creek, Ward Creek, and Meeks Creek watersheds.

Destruction of the watershed inevitably led to habitat loss for many Tahoe mammal and bird species already under pressure from market hunters. Numbers declined drastically, and some species became extinct, extirpated, or temporarily absent such as the California grizzly bear, Sierra Nevada bighorn sheep, Sierra red fox, wolf, sage grouse, and wolverine. Here again, the Tahoe Conflict played out to the disadvantage of the native wildlife in the Tahoe Basin.

Promoters, engineers, and developers have long coveted Lake Tahoe's vast waters as sources of power, navigation, and supply. The first water resource development occurred in 1870 by constructing a wooden buttress dam and gates at the outlet [25] by the Donner Lumber and Boom Co. (DLBC). Water released through the dam gates in surges floated cut logs on the Truckee River downstream to sawmills. In June 1907, an already full Lake Tahoe experienced a one-week 2-foot rise to a record high water of 6,231 feet LTD. LTD stands for Lake Tahoe datum, a reference elevation similar to sea level and used to express the altitude of Lake Tahoe's water surface. The high-water condition overtopped the dam and caused widespread damage to shoreline structures. Armed guards posted at the dam protected it from threatened dynamite attacks by aggrieved lakefront owners.

Export of water from Lake Tahoe was an even bigger prize for entrepreneurial water developers. An early scheme promoted by engineer Alexi von Schmidt began in 1870 by attempting to control the Lake Tahoe outlet and constructing a rock crib diversion dam on the Truckee River about 4 miles below the outlet. From here, von Schmidt proposed an aqueduct and tunnel to supply water to San Francisco. However, the DLBC had already obtained authority directly from the California legislature to construct a dam to control water flow out of the lake that would block von Schmidt's scheme.

The von Schmidt proposal failed due to city fathers' well-founded skepticism and vehement opposition from downstream water users. Ultimately, conflict with the DLBC that controlled the outlet channel doomed the venture.

Again, water developers turned to the Tahoe Basin to augment the dwindling local water supply for Virginia City and Gold Hill's mining boomtowns. Lacking the technology to develop local groundwater supplies or pump water long distances, gravity flow from a distant surface source was the only method to bring water to users. Plentiful water in the Carson Range and Tahoe Basin's upper elevations was high enough (net height of 1,500 feet) to reach the target service area by gravity flow with elevation left over to keep adequate pressure.

Civil engineer Herman Schussler designed brilliantly simple waterworks that would capture water at high elevations. In 1873, the first phase of the project collected water from

Timber buttress dam at the Lake Tahoe outlet, built during 1870 [25]. (*University of Nevada Special Collections*)

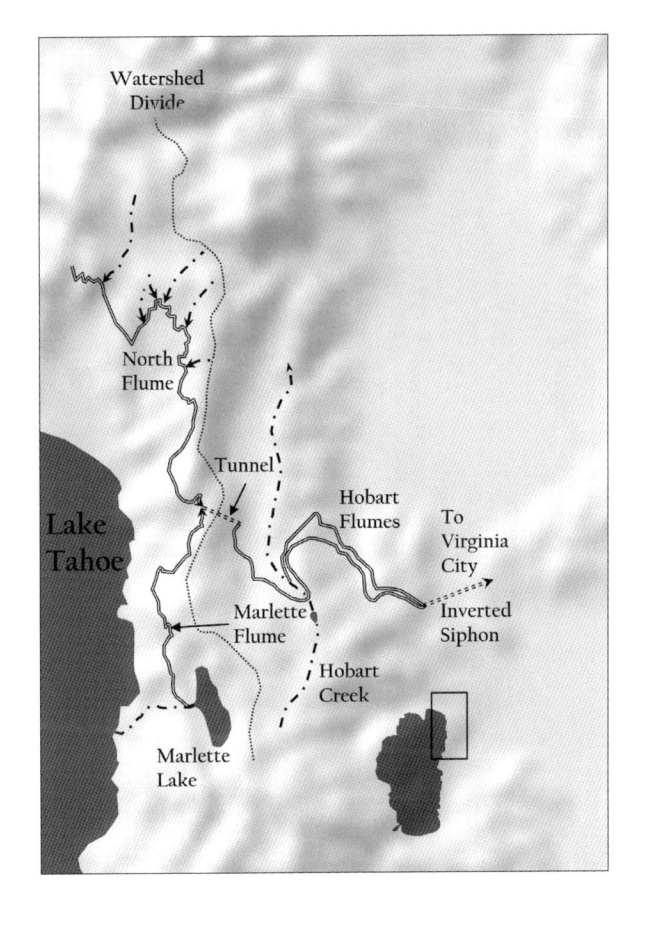

Map of the Virginia City water system in Tahoe.

Hobart Creek on the east slope of the Carson Range and diverted it into a high-pressure wrought iron pipeline. It delivered the water 23 miles across the Nevada desert to the mining towns. This water transmission system required no pumping or added energy input.

The next phase in 1875 extended the water supply source into the Tahoe Basin and added a second transmission pipeline. The aqueducts mentioned earlier in the Sierra Nevada Wood and Lumber Company transport system's description served a dual role as the second phase of the project's water transmission element. The increase of Marlette Lake's capacity occurred at that time, and its water redirected northward into the water system. Water discharged through the tunnel on the Washoe Valley side flowed into an expanded flume and pipeline system. The waterworks had a maximum hydraulic capacity in 1875 of 4.4 million gallons per day on average at total capacity. In its era, this water system was a marvel of its time. It demonstrated extraordinary civil engineering capability in the design and construction of a long-distance all-gravity water system and, for the first time, applied the use of riveted iron pipe at these high pressures.

In western Nevada, the electricity demand spurred the Truckee River General Electric Company to acquire rights at the lake's outlet from Donner Lumber and Boom Company and begin constructing a reinforced concrete slab dam to support new outlet works in 1909 [25]. The new outlet works would raise the average lake level higher than ever before and allow controlled releases to match power demand on the company's hydroelectric generators downstream on the Truckee River.

Simultaneously, as the power company's new outlet works were under construction, the newly created United States Reclamation Service was eyeing the prodigious volume of annual runoff and vast storage capacity of Lake Tahoe. The 1902 Reclamation Act created the Reclamation Service, the forerunner of the current Bureau of Reclamation, within the U.S. Department of Interior. Its mission was to develop cheap water supplies and bring irrigated agriculture to the arid West as an incentive for settlement.

The Reclamation Service began its first project by constructing the Derby Diversion Dam on the Truckee River below Reno in 1905. The dam diverted water to irrigate 206,000 acres in the Lahontan Valley near Fallon, Nevada [26], and deliver political repayment to the Reclamation Act's great benefactor, Nevada Senator Francis Newlands. As a run of the river diversion, it proved unreliable with too little water in the river for needs late in the growing season and insufficient water in dry years. Stored water would be necessary to sustain the irrigated farmlands, and Lake Tahoe was the logical source.

The Reclamation Service and the power company agreed to a friendly condemnation suit resulting in a consent decree that granted an easement for the outlet works to the Reclamation Service in 1915. In exchange, the power company would receive $129,000 for its holdings and guaranteed flows in the Truckee River for hydropower operations. Lake Tahoe would become the centerpiece of its massive Newlands Project for western Nevada and solve the lack of a reliable water supply.

This otherwise seemingly simple transfer of control eventually spawned an assortment of water rights battles among competing parties. Newlands irrigators, existing water users, and tribal interests sought to protect their claimed water rights that, in total, far exceeded

Lake Tahoe Outlet Dam completed in 1913 [25]. (*Wikimedia Commons*)

the available amount of water. The elevation of Lake Tahoe and the amount released into the Truckee River are now under a federal court-appointed watermaster's authority. The watermaster must juggle a hopelessly complex set of rules and mollify rival water interests to achieve a fair and balanced water distribution.

Aside from the ongoing water rights controversy created by the storage of water and downstream diversion, the outlet works' operation inflicted a severe environmental toll. The more obvious impact was the significant change in the Truckee River's natural flow regime, which affected fish migration, destroyed riparian vegetation, caused bank erosion, and killed aquatic life.

The unnaturally elevated lake surface exerted destructive effects on the Lake Tahoe shoreline. Significant shoreline erosion as a source of sediment discharged into the lake continued as the impounded water, and the shoreline fought to reach a new yet unattained equilibrium. The high water drowned out the rare Tahoe yellow cress plant leading to its listing as an endangered species by California and Nevada. Much less obvious was the harmful effects that occurred from the permanent submergence of a partially encircling band of protective vegetation that stabilized the shoreline, offered riparian habitat, and performed natural treatment of runoff directly from adjacent land areas.

In a different scene in the Tahoe Conflict, lakefront homeowners and the Bureau of Reclamation battled each other over Lake Tahoe's level. The lake had no champion representing its existential interests through all of this, and the matter settled in a consensus beneficial to the bureau and lakefront owners.

Downstream, other environments felt the effects of increased water storage in Lake Tahoe in a different way. The diversion of stored water into the Newlands Project choked off the

Photo. No. 1
Taken Aug. 28, 1917.
C.B. Valentine

Tahoe Tavern Casino

Lake elevation (highest for Year) July 17, 1917 = 6229.78
Lake elevation   Aug 28, 1917 = 6229.12

Unnatural shoreline erosion in 1917 near the Tahoe Tavern, Tahoe City [27], caused by the Lake Tahoe Outlet Dam. (*University of Nevada Special Collections*)

flow into Pyramid Lake, the Truckee River's terminus. The lake level dropped approximately 84 feet in the sixty-five years following the onset of diversions into the Newlands Project. Lake Winnemucca, which depended on overflow from Pyramid Lake, dried up. The lowered level of Pyramid Lake caused the exposure of a sand bar at the inlet that blocked the annual migration and spawning of the endangered Lahontan cutthroat and the cui-ui fishes.

Lower and Upper Echo Lakes are a pair of glacially sculpted basins perched on the Sierra Nevada's crest that naturally drain into the Tahoe watershed. In 1876, Pacific Gas and Electric Company's forerunner raised the lakes' level with a new dam and constructed an export pipeline to the American River drainage. The new conduit conveyed water from the Tahoe watershed and into the American River drainage to supplement hydroelectric power production.

An imaginative, if not shocking, *c.* 1918 proposal by the Bureau of Reclamation advanced the thought of raising Lake Tahoe by 20 feet with a higher dam and cutting the rim and outlet channel downward another 20 feet. Here again, water storage for the desired expansion of the Newlands Project was the underlying motive. Water releases would be so high in volume they would flood downstream properties requiring a buyout to prevent lawsuits. The buyout would have included the Lake Tahoe Railway and Transportation Co. railway from Truckee to Tahoe City, effectively cutting off the only convenient access for patronage at their luxury hotel, the Tahoe Tavern (see Chapter 6).

In a terse and imperious statement, the bureau pronounced, "To the extent that we have a prosperous farming community in Nevada dependent upon increase of Tahoe storage, the summer resort and pleasure interests at the Lake will have to yield." Differently, the "Tragedy of the Commons" appears here as a zero-sum economic game; some parties must lose so other parties can win.

The Bliss family cleverly thwarted the bureau's proposal through transactions allowing a Southern Pacific Railroad takeover of their railway and conversion to standard gauge in 1926. Rather than wrestle with the much more powerful SP and the higher costs of condemnation of land, the bureau dropped its plan. Though the Bliss family was motivated by the threat to their Tahoe Tavern hotel, their actions prevented what would have been an irreversible environmental catastrophe.

Nevada interests hatched one final scheme c. 1938 to divert Lake Tahoe through a tunnel beneath the Carson Range that would discharge irrigation water into the Washoe Valley. However, the short-lived plan met von Schmidt's fate when it collided head-on with entrenched opposition from lakefront owners and Truckee River water users.

The geology of the Tahoe Basin does not bear precious metals in enough quantities to justify economic exploitation. Its distance from the gold-mining madness on the Sierra Nevada Mother Lode saved it from nineteenth-century California gold-mining ravages.

Volcanic rocks just north of Lake Tahoe can hold tiny amounts of gold and silver, and on the West Shore, sedimentary rock (ancient seabed) transformed by heat and pressure (metamorphosis) can bear gold. In this latter formation, prospector London L. Noonchester discovered a provable gold deposit in 1932 on the east flank of Ellis Peak. In 1939, he filed a 1,600-acre claim and founded the Tahoe Treasure Mine [28]. A 1947 newspaper article listed on-site employee housing, sawmill, shops, and owner's residence with a workforce of twenty employees. The news story quoted an overly enthusiastic Noonchester predicting a lode value of $50 million. Noonchester ran the Lake Tahoe Gold Mining Company intermittently, and 1960 Winter Olympics organizers used his claim temporarily for cross-country ski trails. Eventually, the U.S. Forest Service bought the land thinking it would prevent further environmental damage by subsequent mining activity. In this case, it was a move that served as a harbinger of the coming shift toward the Tahoe Conflict's protection side. However, a loophole in the General Mining Law of 1872 still allows filing of mineral claims, though actual hard rock mining is all but impossible under current regional land use rules.

Between 1897 and 1918, at least four legislative attempts to confer federal forest reserve or national park protection onto the Tahoe Basin failed. Landowner opposition and public outcry led by legendary nineteenth-century conservationist John Muir, who decried the windfall benefits to timber companies, sealed the fate of at least three attempts.

It was not until 1899 that tangible action in forest conservation occurred. That year, President William McKinley signed legislation moving 135,355 acres into the Lake Tahoe Forest Reserve. In 1907, the forest reserves became national forests. This action was a decisive move that set into motion a conservation ethic for Tahoe's forests. It was a small but meaningful win for the future as the Tahoe Conflict raged on. Today, the U.S. Forest Service protects 78 percent of the land in the Tahoe Basin as a national forest.

A final significant attempt for national park status occurred in 1935 when the U.S. Department of Interior evaluated the area. Though the environment was improving, the abused land, widespread private ownership of the shoreline, and high land values led the department to reject it as unworthy of national park designation. Ironically, it still had many scenic qualities and recreation opportunities that made it a highly valued natural resource and a desirable place to live and visit.

Perhaps this was an inverted example of humans' ability to change the environment exceeding their ability to foresee these changes' effects. Here, well-intentioned Department of Interior officials could neither appreciate Lake Tahoe's ecological distinctiveness and value nor envision the potential for harmful change. National Park officials did not sufficiently understand the uniqueness of the lake's combination of volume, depth, altitude, and clarity, nor did science fully understand the fragility of the lake's ecology and its sensitivity to even minute amounts of pollution. They declined to make the decision that would have secured its future.

As this era ended, the Tahoe environment staggered from many impacts based on the resource extraction and exploitation economy. These impacts fully taxed the watershed's regenerative ability to restore the denuded forests and rangelands though aided by an abrupt halt in these environmentally harmful activities. In other areas, such as damming and water diversions, the impacts would be ongoing, or the resource depleted or damaged beyond recovery, as in the native fishery. In every Tahoe Conflict confrontation during this era, the Tahoe environment soundly lost out to private interests and societal advancement.

6

SEASONAL DESTINATION TOURISM (1890–1930)

The inherent and irresistible magnetic draw of Tahoe as a leisure and recreation destination started a scant sixteen years after its discovery by the outside world. A few people built small fishing cabins or rustic hunting lodges, such as Pioneer Stage Lines owner Ben Holladay's lodge in Emerald Bay. However, it would take improved access and personal wealth to avail oneself of the wonders of nineteenth-century Lake Tahoe.

As a primary benefit of socio-economic advancement among the upper class, growing numbers of Americans found themselves with the time and economic resources to tour, sightsee, relax, luxuriate, recuperate, socialize, explore, recreate, and retreat. Tahoe became their preferred choice. First, it achieved popularity as a regional destination for the growing upper class that arose from nearby economies based on mineral wealth and resource exploitation. Tahoe attracted more significant numbers of affluent visitors throughout the nation as the industrial revolution's quality-of-life advancements spread across America. Transportation improvements such as railroads and cruise ships now made long-distance travel safe, efficient, and economical. Summering at Tahoe was a sign of wealth and social status. Being at Tahoe was not as important as being seen at Tahoe and having it reported in your hometown society column.

In a cleverly contrived appeal to nationalistic pride, commercial interests encouraged Americans to visit places of extraordinary beauty and pay homage to exemplary American industrial prowess. In the European Grand Tour tradition as a coming-of-age ritual, they implored Americans to "See America First" (before traveling to Europe) as an act of patriotism. Tahoe uniquely met both criteria and was on the "must-see list."

The earliest resorts were simply hotels fitted to a higher quality than a nearby roadhouse and supplemented by the desired amenities such as lodging, meals, dancing, strolling, sightseeing, and card games. Other establishments functioned as hunting and fishing lodges, such as McKinney's, offering expert guide services together with accommodations befitting a "gentleman sportsman." In Tahoe City, the Grand Central Hotel was reputed to

The rustic McKinney's Lodge, *c.* 1886, by R. J. Waters [14]. (*University of Nevada Special Collections*)

Grand Central Hotel in Tahoe City [25] in 1875 by Carleton Watkins. (*Getty Museum*)

Lucky Baldwin's Tallac House [28], *c.* 1915, with the "hotel-casino" on the left, boathouse in the center, and the service pier and pavilion to the far right. (*Putnam & Valentine postcard*)

be the finest between San Francisco and Virginia City in the latter 1800s and served as an early transportation hub for stage lines and steamships.

A few promoted the Tahoe environment's healthful qualities as a cure for everything from the common cold to "consumption," an archaic term for then-incurable tuberculosis, accompanied by progressive wasting of the body. The "germ theory" of disease transmission had yet to reach acceptance, and widespread belief was that disease was caused by "bad air," known as miasma. What better place to inhale from an atmosphere that Mark Twain extolled in 1872, "The air up there in the clouds is very pure and fine, bracing and delicious. And why shouldn't it be?—it is the same the angels breathe."

In the 1880s, Elias "Lucky" Baldwin's luxurious Tallac House [28] on 1,000 acres of untouched land along the South Shore embodied some of the best in the West's accommodations and service. The hotel catered to the wealthy and featured amenities such as a spring-loaded dance floor, strolling paths, and a casino.

With the advent of stagecoach service in 1857, travel to Tahoe for pleasure became more comfortable. Stagecoaches and wagons served as the transit system over primitive roads and beaches when the water level was low. The Central Pacific Railway's advancement over the Sierra Nevada by April 1868 and its transcontinental connection in 1869 brought modern transit as close as Truckee. Tourists could now ride the railway at greater distances, saving precious travel time and effort. A 15-mile stagecoach ride from rail depot in Truckee and along the scenic Truckee River brought travelers to the Tahoe Basin gateway at Tahoe City. Once at Tahoe City, the most preferred travel choice was the steamship for those headed to other destinations around the lake. Steamers were an integral part of the Tahoe resort experience as an elegant mode of transportation in addition to meeting the more mundane duties of hauling freight and delivering mail.

In parallel with early resort development, the wealthiest families of San Francisco, Sacramento, and Virginia City were building luxury estates. Land moguls, financial tycoons, newspaper publishers, corporate chieftains, and affluent heirs acquired large tracts of recovering lakefront land from logging interests. They turned these lands into palatial estates for summer living and entertaining and became the center of Tahoe summer society. They gave a respite from the fog-shrouded San Francisco Peninsula and relief from the Sacramento Valley and Western Nevada's oppressive heat. A staff of servants prepared sumptuous meals, handled housekeeping duties, and organized recreational and social activities while treating fortunate guests like royalty.

The history of the Ehrman Family estate exemplifies the typical lifestyle of the wealthy in turn-of-the-century Tahoe. Constructed in 1902 by San Francisco financier and family patriarch Isaias W. Hellman, Pine Lodge [29] was one of the largest and most renowned estates. It was 11,703 sq. feet of superb craftsmanship situated on 1,016 acres with 2 miles of shoreline near Tahoma. In later years, similar elaborate mansions appeared, such as Vikingsholm [30], Thunderbird Lodge, and Valhalla, all of which survive to this day.

A visit to Pine Lodge was both a delightful treat and a formal expectation. The family would entertain as many as fifty guests during the summer season. Mornings began at 10 a.m. with breakfast served in bed. Guests could stroll the grounds, relax on the porch, play billiards, or boat on the lake in the Ehrman's wooden powerboat, the *Cherokee*.

Juices and *hors d'oeuvres* were available throughout the day. At 7 p.m., the butler served cocktails on the porch. Dinner in formal attire was at 7:30 p.m. with each guest's needs attended by the butler.

Just as he foresaw the strong market for lumber in Virginia City, visionary timber baron Duane L. Bliss presciently saw the mega-shift to destination tourism. His vision was all-encompassing and remarkably efficient at generating income from the customer, even when measured by today's standards. Anecdotally, twenty cents of every dollar brought to Tahoe found its way into Bliss' hands. His new business venture would serve the guest with a high-quality experience and include transportation, lodging, meals, personal services, retail items, and leisure activities.

Modern photo of Pine Lodge, the former Hellman–Ehrman Mansion at Ed Z'berg Sugar Pine Point State Park. (*Wikimedia Commons*)

Modern photo of Vikingsholm at Emerald Bay [30]. (*Visit California*)

The guest would lack nothing and have no reason to leave Bliss enterprises' care during their stay. When it opened for business in 1902, Bliss' Tahoe Tavern [27] in Tahoe City was the gold standard of the Tahoe resort experience and one of the finest hotels west of the Mississippi.

As the Glenbrook mills shut down in 1897, Bliss began moving trusted personnel, construction materials, buildings, railroad rolling stock and rails, and machinery to his new center of operations at Tahoe City.

He commissioned one of his five sons, an architect, to design a grand resort hotel that would rival accommodations elsewhere in the nation. Another son, a civil engineer, was to survey and plan a narrow-gauge railway connection between the Southern Pacific mainline in Truckee and Tahoe City to reuse the logging company's salvaged railroad assets. Bliss ordered the construction of a luxury steamer that he launched in 1896. Christened the SS *Tahoe* by Bliss's grandson, the vessel would become a timeless icon of the Tahoe resort industry's luxury. Fittingly, a descendant of Tahoe City's founding family, the Pomins, would be its venerable captain.

Bliss captured the multimodal transit system end to end. Guests of the Tahoe Tavern and other resorts would travel by train to Truckee on the Southern Pacific Railway. They would transfer to the Bliss-owned narrow-gauge railway that carried them 15 miles on a scenic Truckee River ride to Tahoe City. If staying at the Tahoe Tavern, guests would step off in front of the hotel's grand entrance. The train would then carry through-travel passengers to the pier, where they would disembark. Walking a few feet across the dock, they would board the waiting steamer SS *Tahoe* to continue their journey to another lakefront resort or estate. To return, guests and travelers reversed their incoming itineraries.

Postcard image of the Tahoe Tavern, *c.* 1911 by Harold Parker [27]. (*University of Nevada Special Collections*)

Left: Tahoe Tavern veranda's [27] view and solitude enjoyed by a lone guest in 1906. (*University of Nevada Special Collections*)

Below: Steamer SS *Tahoe* in the early twentieth century. (*University of Nevada Special Collections*)

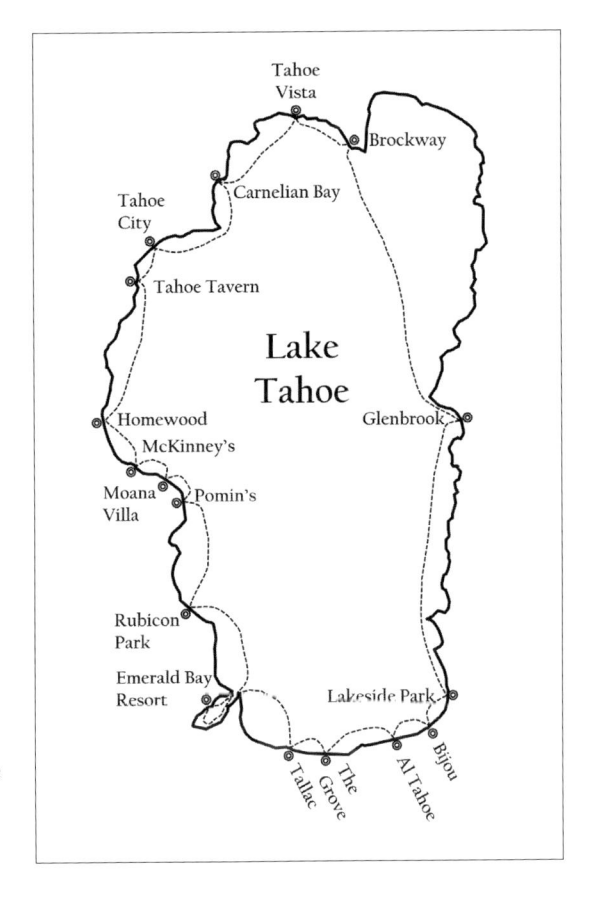

Right: SS *Tahoe*'s course and ports of call on its seasonal daily 72-mile circumnavigation of Lake Tahoe.

Below: SS *Tahoe* and train of the Lake Tahoe Railway & Transportation Co. transferring passengers on the Tahoe Tavern pier, *c.* 1905 [27]. (*Stanley Palmer, University of Nevada Special Collections*)

By 1915, twenty-one major destination resorts encircled the lake or existed in its back-country. Accommodations varied, but it was typically a room with indoor plumbing and included meals. A few locations offered a more rustic experience with tent cabins and meals in an outdoor dining hall. Brockway Hot Springs and Glen Alpine offered natural springs with purported medicinal benefits. Most resorts offered excursions out on the lake for fishing and sightseeing and horseback trips into the backcountry. A few had dance halls, and most featured shaded verandas or patios under the trees for sitting, relaxing, and playing cards.

Over the next four decades, Tahoe visitors enjoyed the best luxury in any number of quality destination resorts. If ever there was a time that Tahoe would resemble a modern national park, it was then. Minimal impact tourist accommodations, a well-developed transit system, limited roadway development, large tracts of open space, minimal commercial enterprises, a recovering forest, improving lake health, scenic vistas, and no vehicle air pollution—these characteristics would have made it the embodiment of a national park comparable to any Yosemite or Yellowstone of today.

Despite its natural and unspoiled ambiance, the era was not environmentally benign. The absence of community sewer systems meant resorts with indoor plumbing piped raw human waste directly into the lake. The lake's immense volume and the relatively low wastewater flow made dilution an effective solution. Also, up until 1915, people believed it was impossible to float in Lake Tahoe and only went wading waist-deep if they entered the lake at all. Most experienced the lake from the safety of a boat or steamer. This combination of factors prevented water contact that allows disease transmission from the untreated human waste discharges into water bodies. A sanitary survey in the 1930s found evidence of ongoing sewage pollution.

Most resorts used gravity water supply systems fed by uphill springs and upstream surface water diversions. The disposal of human waste did not contaminate these sources, although naturally occurring microbes could have been problematic if resort owners did not disinfect the supply.

Solid waste was dumped away from hotels or barged out onto the lake for disposal. It was customary to dump waste into flowing watercourses that would carry away the trash. The Tahoe Tavern did both. Again, the lake's water volume and the small seasonal waste load were factors in keeping this unsanitary practice from becoming a nuisance.

During the Great Depression and the advent of World War II, Tahoe would languish, vulnerable to future impactful change, good or bad. From the viewpoint of the twenty-first century, we would come to view this era as the Golden Age of Tahoe, a romanticized ideal of what we could have had now, a sentimental time to relive, and a warm memory of nostalgic ambiance long gone and perhaps, forever lost.

7

Rise of Automobile Tourism (1910–1960)

The first appearance of automobiles began in the early twentieth century as adventurous motorists sought to test their mettle and prove the auto's worth on roads intended to handle animal drawn wagon traffic. As the automobile gained popularity and became an essential convenience, Tahoe resorts had no choice but to change or fall behind.

The sudden appearance of an automobile in 1905 at Tallac House [28] portended a new variable in the tourism equation. Tourism promoters seized the car's improved tourist mobility and sponsored contests for the first automobile to reach Lake Tahoe each season. The automobile brought the concept of vacationing to even more significant numbers through the economy and freedom afforded by this new form of independent transportation. As the car conquered Tahoe, the infrastructure and economy responded. Governments pursued an aggressive roadway construction program, followed closely by a new resort business model that now catered to a rapidly expanding middle class, drive-up market.

The completion of the road around Emerald Bay in 1913 and the Lincoln Highway route's adoption launched the "Wishbone Route" promotion through Tahoe. A triangle of roads formed the route—Lake Tahoe Wagon Road, the new West Shore Road to the Truckee (River) Turnpike, and Lincoln Highway over Donner Summit—with its apex in Sacramento.

Rudimentary auto and wagon roads ringed Tahoe in 1914, except the driving distance between Glenbrook and present-day Incline Village. During this period, barges carried summer automobile traffic across the lake between Tahoe City and Glenbrook.

August 1925 marked the completion of the missing East Shore roadway segment between Glenbrook and Incline. Autos could now circumnavigate the lake solely on land. Highway officials elevated the old Lake Tahoe Wagon Road to highway status as U.S. Highway 50 in 1927. Significant roadway improvements followed in quick succession culminating in the paving of all Tahoe Basin main roads by 1935. The year 1947 marked the completion of paved all-weather two-lane highways leading into the basin. The California Division of Highways

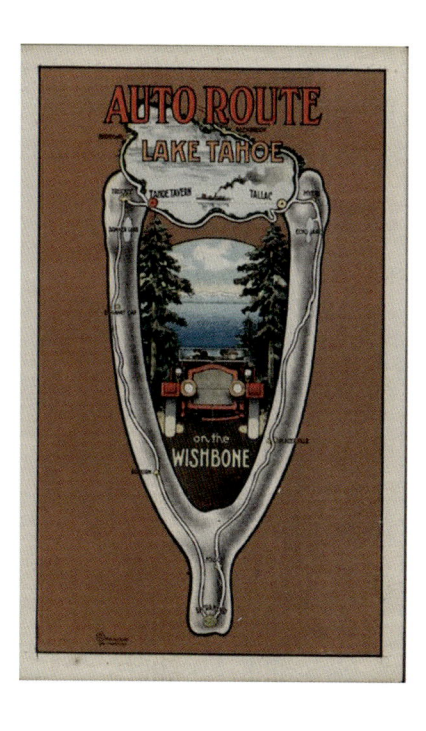

Postcard promoting the Wishbone
Autoroute through Lake Tahoe, *c.* 1919.
(*De Macrae collection Public Domain*)

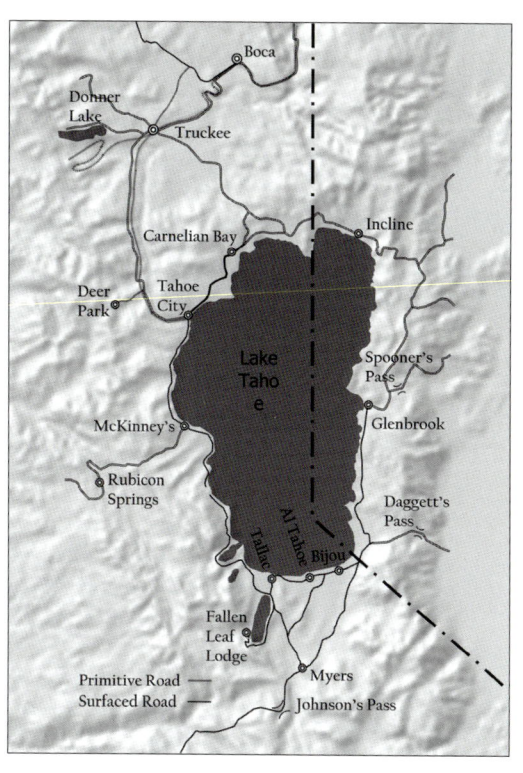

Roads and common destinations in the
Tahoe region in 1915 (after *The Lake of the
Sky* by G. W. James).

accelerated all-weather Interstate 80 to substantial completion between Sacramento and Truckee in time for the 1960 Winter Olympics, and the extension to Reno finished in 1964.

The classic venerable destination resorts faced daunting challenges of advanced age, cultural obsolescence, and socio-economic shifts. A rapidly expanding middle-class clientele looked for a more economical, family-oriented, and value-filled vacation experience. The trend toward car-friendly campgrounds and bargained priced "auto courts" effectively targeted the newly mobile market segment. Gradually, the classic posh destination resorts lapsed into a state of decay.

Southern Pacific dismantled the idle Truckee to Tahoe City railway and sold rolling stock to collectors and rails for scrap beginning in 1941. Owners scuttled or scavenged obsolete old steamers and auctioned off well-worn furnishings. The classic resorts faded out and were razed and reborn as condominium complexes and exclusive second home enclaves in the ensuing era. Developers demolished the revered Tahoe Tavern to make way for pricey lakefront condominiums in 1963. Other resorts and estates following the same fate were Moana Villa, Chambers Landing, Pomin's, Fleur du Lac, Stanley Dollar Estate, and Globin's Al Tahoe, among many others. Ironically, the last classic resort to go under was the Glenbrook Inn in 1976, as it later remerged remodeled into a condominium building surrounded by upscale home sites behind a guarded gate. The automobile had prevailed once again.

A few cherished examples of the old resorts and estates survived through state and federal agencies' rescue efforts in the 1960s and 1970s. The U.S. Forest Service acquired Baldwin's Tallac Resort grounds and the stately homes of Tevis, McGonagle, and Pope to create the Tallac Historic Site. They brought Camp Richardson, Bay View Resort, Zephyr Cove Resort, Round Hill Pines Resort, Meeks Bay Resort, and Angora Lakes Resort into public ownership and preservation. California State Parks acquired the estates and large tracts at Pine Lodge on Sugar Pine Point, Vikingsholm in Emerald Bay, Skylandia Lodge on the North Shore, and the old Tahoe Dam Gatekeepers Cabin at Tahoe City.

The California legislature appropriated money to purchase Henry Kaiser's rustic Fleur du Lac estate, but California Governor Ronald Reagan vetoed the transaction in a myopic spending cut. The U.S. Forest Service acquired the reclusive George Whittell's 10,000 acres on the East Shore. The lodge remained in a financial tycoon's private ownership and was eventually obtained and transferred to the exclusive Thunderbird Preservation Society. The Tahoe Conflict seesawed back and forth as benign "Old Tahoe" development either moved into preservation status or razed and replaced by more impactful modern buildings.

The 1930s and post-World War II Tahoe saw private campgrounds, motels, and commercial services spring up as more visitors poured into the basin in cars packed with expanding families. The next mega-shift in tourism was well underway. All new development would now conform to the automobile's demands—large parking lots, spread-out services, and sprawling strip commercial zones—all conveniently served by an increasing network of all-season roads. The newly created impervious surfaces accumulated fine sediment, nutrients, trash, deicing chemicals, and organic particles. The tailpipes spewed tons of nitrogen-based compounds that descended into the lake at night. The runoff from hard

Early automobile family camping at Tahoe
in 1916. (*1916 Shoreline Photographic Survey*)

surfaces and tailpipe emissions became an additional source of pollution that flowed
unabated into streams and the lake, contributing to the loss of clarity.

It was early in the beginning of this era that the effects of climate change would begin
to stimulate subtle but harmful changes in the Tahoe environment. Due to the absence
of systematic monitoring and lack of scientific knowledge about the lake, these gradual
changes and the harm caused would go unnoticed until the later part of the twentieth
century. It is not lost on many that the rise of local automobile tourism and the worldwide
increase in greenhouse gases expelled into the atmosphere are an ironic coincidence.

After its growth heyday of 1910–1960, one can easily observe that the era of automobile
tourism continues with strength and without any indication of a significant near-term
decrease in volume or replacement by alternative forms of transportation. Roughly 80
percent of visitors still arrive at Tahoe in an individual vehicle. Local governments attempt
to decrease the miles traveled in the basin by offering rudimentary transit, mostly involving
seasonal and event-related buses and shuttles while encouraging bike transportation.

Turning away from Tahoe's dependence on the automobile will not be easy, nor will it
happen quickly. The configuration of much of the private and commercial built environment
is to cater to the car. Changing this will require innovative solutions that make alternative
forms of transportation more attractive and preserve the viability of destinations now
served by the automobile.

8

Resort Development Boom and Year-Round Tourism (1960–2002)

In the mid-twentieth century, tourist activity options expanded into even more areas beyond traditional summer outdoor recreation pursuits and socializing. The arrival of large-scale, casino style gaming tarnished the wholesome Tahoe image, put extreme demands on housing and infrastructure, and needed a year round resident workforce. In contrast, the mid-twentieth-century car camping rage seemed perfect for the open public lands and rustic seasonal resorts and campgrounds that sprang up. Meanwhile, the post-war California economy boomed, and its attendant benefits created explosive population growth, more disposable income, and increased leisure time for a new and upwardly mobile middle class. Superimposed on all of this was the addition of a rapidly expanding and culturally unique wintertime recreation economy. Tahoe would enter a phase of unrestricted, intense, and environmentally harmful residential and commercial development that would span four environmentally traumatic decades.

Tahoe had been an exclusive enclave for the wealthy who could afford to construct self-sustaining seasonal estates on large tracts in the preceding era. As access improved, developers laid out summer-only subdivisions of low-priced small lots suitable for a platform tent or a simple one-room cabin. Dirt roads, summer-only water systems, pit privies, cesspools, and septic tanks served these early seasonal communities, many of which clustered around the old resorts or a commercial center.

In the 1920s and 1930s, both ends of the lake saw new low-key seasonal home tracts, particularly around the sleepy communities of Lake Valley, Tahoe City, Lake Forest, Kings Beach, Tahoe Vista, and Crystal Bay. The 1940s were a respite from significant subdivision activity, but the number of residences still doubled to 3,081. The 1930s and 1940s were still a time of summer pleasure only for the well-to-do.

A popular activity was watching the captains of industry engaging in summer motorboat racing, each trying to outdo the other. The growth pressure was low, and although these new second home tracts ignored most environmental protections, they were lacking in number and density and distant from each other.

Early twentieth-century rustic cabin in Kings Beach [31]. (*University of Nevada Special Collections*)

In the late 1950s and the excitement leading up to the 1960 Winter Olympics, the upswing in winter sports participation, principally downhill skiing, added a second season to the always dicey summer tourism economy. What had been a quirky winter pastime among locals and elites elsewhere in isolated winter communities was now entering widespread popularity. This second mega-shift in tourism catapulted Tahoe into an exclusive international class of resort areas that accommodated the upscale winter sports enthusiast and added untold value to existing resort properties.

The Tahoe Tavern had experimented with winter recreation in the 1920s, but it amounted to little more than a bobsleigh run, cross-country ski trails, and snow play areas. The region submitted an unsuccessful bid for the 1932 Winter Olympics, losing out to Lake Placid, NY.

Despite losing the Olympic bid, the community pressed ahead with its winter sports dreams, adding a ski jump and hosting the United States Olympic western ski jumping and cross-country trials in 1931. The industry gained traction with the opening of the Sugar Bowl Ski Area just west of Donner Summit in 1939 and, about the same time, White Hills on Spooner Summit. A revival of the Tahoe Tavern site as Granlibakken Ski Area [32] followed in 1947. Eventual winter sports behemoths Palisades Tahoe [33] first spun its lift in 1949, and Heavenly Valley Ski Area (Heavenly Mountain Resort) [34] followed in 1956.

The televised ski events of the 1960 Winter Olympics [33] [35] created a higher awareness of skiing as a recreational sport. It boosted the modern western ski industry that was already on its way to more than doubling day-use. New ski areas emerged, including such luminaries as Alpine Meadows (1961), Mt. Rose (1964), and upscale destination resort

The Disney-designed Tower of Nations, Flame Cauldron, and Tribune of Honor for the 1960 Winter Olympics [33]. The sculptures were made of wire, papier-mâché, and stucco and razed following the games. (© *Bill Briner, Used by Permission*)

Northstar-at-Tahoe (1972). Inside and outside the Tahoe Basin, existing mom-and-pop ski areas expanded to meet the increased demand.

The western ski industry acquired new participants at a spirited pace in the 1960s and early 1970s, and Tahoe was its ground zero. Over twelve years, ever-increasing numbers of skiers visited Tahoe resorts. South Shore ski areas saw a 231 percent overall increase in skier visits, but their North Shore competitors overshadowed them, increasing twice that—461 percent. By 2006, skier and snowboarder visits among Southwestern U.S. ski areas would reach a peak. A slow decline followed, but Tahoe managed to stay flat.

Due to the staging of the 1960 Winter Olympics at the dawn of the resort development boom era, one could think that the event was the cause of the increase in growth and land development. However, that would be a *post hoc* logical fallacy by assuming a cause-and-effect relationship between the two. At best, we can only say the Olympics ignited a short-lived localized boomlet and accelerated by ten years the onset of development pressures that were inevitable anyway.

The period of 1970–1990 was a period of growth throughout the Sierra Nevada, an era known as the "Second Gold Rush." California grew 49 percent during that time, and the whole of the Sierra Nevada saw 130 percent growth. For example, unincorporated Nevada County, where no Olympics occurred, grew by 260 percent. Truckee saw its first growth spurt in eighty years, with 150 percent growth triggered by the massive Tahoe Donner subdivision. Meanwhile, the Tahoe Basin population increased 103 percent during the same twenty-year period. Considering the influx of seasonal residents and visitors into the Tahoe Basin in addition to residents, the already high peak day population increased 14.6 percent over the same period. With the rapid rise of gaming and winter sports and its drive-up customer base, one could misperceive from the expanded built environment that Tahoe grew faster than other mountain areas.

In 1931, Nevada legalized what we now call casino-style gambling. Up until the late 1950s, just across the California–Nevada state line, a few rustic gambling parlors eked out a living from summer visitors who had come to Tahoe for other reasons and could not resist the temptation. From an inauspicious start as bingo parlors and card rooms, the industry shook off its social stigma, characterized itself as "gaming" instead of gambling, and associated itself with fantasy themes of wealth, luxury, celebrity, glamour, and sensuality.

Known as the "Lady of the Lake," the elegant but shady Cal Neva Casino in Crystal Bay [36], Nevada, began as a private vacation retreat in 1926. The lodge became a casino in the 1930s, following the sale to new owners. A fire in 1937 leveled the structure, and owners quickly rebuilt it. Several smaller seasonal casinos joined it nearby in the 1940s, and they too struggled through economic downturns and ownership changes. The Cal Neva became a favorite haunt of gangsters and the elite throughout the 1940s and 1950s. Frank Sinatra and partners acquired the buildings in 1960 and remodeled and expanded with a showroom and hotel tower. Sinatra lost his gambling license in 1963 because of association with known criminal figures and divested himself of the property. What followed was a controversial series of owners, bankruptcies, and scandals that culminated in the facility's closure in 2013. Despite purchase in early 2018 by tech mogul and real estate investor Larry Ellison, its future remains uncertain.

Meanwhile, at Stateline, NV, on the south end of the lake, butcher and restaurateur Harvey Gross and former Reno bingo parlor owner William F. Harrah took casino gaming to its highest levels. As is true in any nascent industry, it is the larger-than-life visionaries that create the reality. Each man thought big and made risky bets that legendary adverse weather conditions and distance from urban centers would not deter the drive-up gambler.

Gross opened his casino [37] in 1956, followed across the street by Harrah's [37] in 1957. In the 1970s, both casinos underwent major expansions with the addition of multi-story hotel towers. Other major casino players entered the South Shore market—Del Webb's Sahara Tahoe [37] in 1965 and the Park Cattle Company's Park Tahoe [37] in 1978, both with multistory hotel towers.

Aerial view of Stateline area in 1940. The dashed area is where the casino and hotel core would emerge. (*Google Earth*)

Aerial view of Stateline area in 2020 showing the casino and hotel core [37]. (*Google Earth*)

The direct and indirect environmental impacts of dense high-rise casino development were both profoundly penetrating and far-reaching at the same time. The casinos at Stateline created the demand for thousands of workers who sought affordable housing and strained public services such as schools, utility systems, law enforcement, and social welfare programs. For example, Stateline casinos employed 13,000 workers in 1990. These impacts happened mainly on the California side, where the closest affordable housing concentration existed. A marginally viable casino zone continued at the North Shore, and despite similar impacts, they were minuscule compared to the massive gaming development on the South Shore. Heavy incoming automobile traffic headed for the casino core, often backed up for 5 or more miles westward on Highway 50 into California. The result was prolonged periods of persistent congestion and gridlock during the summer and winter holidays, smothered by unhealthful air quality from idling vehicles.

The Stateline gaming complex was a maddening circumstance where Nevada's interests solely benefited from the business but shifted the costly social, transportation, and environmental impacts to California. It was a classic example of a "Tragedy of the Commons" lopsided transaction with one side receiving all the benefits (profits) but spreading the negative consequences (social and environmental costs) to others.

The year 1960 marked the beginning of a dramatic upswing in the Tahoe growth curve. The natural beauty and recreational opportunities have always made Tahoe attractive, and this period marked a convergence of many new factors that boosted the growth curve. The central factors were explosive population growth and a strong economy in post-war California, increased disposable income, more available leisure time, ease of access in automobiles over all-weather roads, large tracts of private land suitable for development, affordable resort accommodations, lax environmental rules, and cultural interest in nature as an escape from the pressures of urban life.

The onslaught of public demand and politically skilled land developers overwhelmed local governments. Politically conservative pro-growth elected officials embedded in the construction, real estate, and retail industries dominated local government. They were unwilling or unable to conduct sensible and coordinated planning to resist the sizeable economic benefits that development would bestow upon their communities. Local elected officials at the time adhered to a pro-property rights philosophy that elevated these individual rights above the basic human right to a healthy environment free of degradation. It manifested itself in decisions that granted harmful projects a go-ahead and gave developers a pass on installing costly environmental protection measures. Here we saw the "Tragedy of the Commons" play out as each local agency did what it thought best for itself without regard to cumulative and regional impacts.

As development progressed, concerns about wastewater discharge within the Tahoe Basin began to arise in the 1950s. Domestic wastewater carries significant loads of organic matter, suspended solids, nutrients, and pathogenic bacteria. The nitrogen and phosphorus nutrients movement from on-site individual waste disposal systems threatened the lake by rapidly increasing algae growth. Some communities had sewers for public health reasons but discharged the treated wastewater to ponds and spray fields, allowing the nutrient-rich effluent to migrate into the lake anyway.

A 1963 report produced by the Lake Tahoe Area Council addressed the issue squarely. The report said protecting fragile Lake Tahoe required connecting all habitable structures to a sewer system and exporting the treated wastewater to areas outside of the Tahoe Basin. What followed were individual on-site waste disposal system prohibitions embedded into state and federal law. These were the California Porter-Cologne Act of 1970, Nevada governor's 1969 executive order banning septic tanks after 1972, and the Federal Clean Water Act of 1972. Millions of dollars in government grants and low-interest loans flowed into massive public works projects needed for sewering and export mandate compliance.

Advanced water reclamation plant constructed by the Tahoe-Truckee Sanitation Agency in 1976-77 for $20 million with the Truckee River shown in the lower-left corner [38]. (*TTSA*)

The massive sewering of the Tahoe Basin paradoxically prevented and created environmental damage. The removal of wastewater discharges away from the lake was no doubt a positive move. However, few realized the growth-inducing impact it would bring. A 1974 Environmental Protection Agency report laid out this argument: environmental problems at Lake Tahoe result from inadequate land-use planning and the growth-inducing influence of sewerage systems. As the idea went, sewers allowed for higher-density and more widespread development than without.

As a compromise of the Tahoe Conflict's opposing forces, the EPA would only fund existing demand in future grants and would not include grant-funded sewerage capacity for unapproved future growth.

The seminal Lake Tahoe Area Council 1963 report marked the beginning of an in-depth and sustained scientific research effort into the lake and its relationship with the watershed. A contributor of an appendix to that report was a low-profile but articulate and passionate assistant professor at UC Davis with a Ph.D. in limnology (the study of lakes and other freshwater bodies), Professor Charles R. Goldman. He later emerged as the leading scientific force in the movement to protect the lake. He would serve as the oracle of science-based information to support growth policies and land-use decisions to stem the coming surge of pollution threatening the lake.

In 1968, Goldman formed the Tahoe Research Group from professors, highly skilled technicians, and an army of graduate students. Working initially from Davis and in cabins at Tahoe, they later established a laboratory in an abandoned fish hatchery building near Tahoe City. Goldman and his team conducted primary research into the lake's physical, chemical, and biological characteristics from this modest start. They produced a significant body of ground-breaking technical papers. This salvo of credible research shaped public policy on the lake over the next fifty-plus years and stymied the early pro-growth forces who were helpless to counter the well-documented conclusions and warnings.

Subdivision development was in full swing by the late 1950s. During the 1950s and 1960s, new tracts appeared on the West Shore, North Shore, Southeast Shore, Upper Truckee Marsh, Lake Valley, and Christmas Valley, all significantly denser given the forthcoming availability of community sewers. In the 1970s, developers targeted the upscale market with 9,000 new lots in Incline Village [39] that could not have occurred without its sewers, treatment plant, and export pipeline. California banned new subdivisions in 1975, and regional planners imposed a ban on new subdivisions throughout the basin in 1980. By that time, some 49,000 subdivided lots over 28,000 acres were in existence or held approvals.

Subdivisions exert a wide range of environmental impacts on the Tahoe Basin. Road construction and grading for structures remove stabilizing vegetation and cause the erosion of disturbed soil surfaces. Grading, filling, and channelization destroyed stream environment zones (creeks, meadows, and marshes) that acted as natural pollution filters. Paved roads, driveways, roofs, and patios contribute to runoff that carries petroleum products, fine sediment particles, pet feces, and spilled chemicals into the lake. Landscaping consumes water, introduces non-native and invasive plant species, and needs fertilizers that add to the lake's nutrient loading. Depending on location, wildlife habitat disappeared, and natural migration corridors became blocked. Wastewater systems became overloaded, at times resulting in massive spillages of sewage and bans on new connections. Inadequate state highways became overloaded with owners and tenants entering and exiting adjoining subdivisions. For example, miles-long seasonal and holiday traffic jams often occurred on roads leading into and out of Tahoe City. A similar 5-mile-long eastbound traffic jam clogged Highway 50 during the peak summer and winter holiday months.

During the early to mid-1970s, intense growth occurred in the construction of single-family dwellings. The real estate and construction industries turned to still largely unregulated single-family second homes on the vast inventory of vacant previously approved subdivision lots to meet the burgeoning demand. An army of realtors sold these lots to buyers who intended one of two outcomes—retire to Tahoe on their dream lot or retire off Tahoe by speculating that the property would sell at a highly appreciated price. Many of these were second homes and investment properties built on the expected purchase by out-of-town buyers.

One subdivision deserves special attention—Tahoe Keys [40]. Begun in 1957 by Dillingham Development Company, Tahoe Keys became the poster child for unenlightened land-use planning and ignorance about the watershed's value. In fairness to Dillingham, the 1950s were not when the throttling of growth for environmental reasons was popular or even thought to be necessary. Like the one from which Tahoe Keys emerged, land planners viewed marshes as swampy wastelands and nuisances. In this case, the swamp was the wetland outlet of Trout Creek and the Upper Truckee River, the largest tributary to Lake Tahoe.

The "Keys," its common name, are the peninsulas of buildable land formed by dredging. The developer used the excavated materials to build up dry land bounded on each side by shallow lagoons created by the excavation. An open channel allowed direct vessel access and hydrologic connectivity to Lake Tahoe. Completed in 1975, the project created 1,451 new lots and a marina on 500 acres with 12 miles of prime waterfront property where there was only about one mile in the beginning. Again, it would have been an impossible project without access to community sewers.

The Tahoe Keys' construction inflicted all the usual impacts of land development at Lake Tahoe, plus a few more exotic problems related to the exchange of its waters with Lake Tahoe. In the summer months, the lagoons held warmed stagnant water that became a breeding ground for insect swarms, produced foul odors, supported rooted aquatic plants, and degraded water quality. In recent years, invasive warm-water fish such as goldfish and bass became established in the Keys' lagoons. Invasive mollusks such as Asian clams and invasive aquatic plants such a curly-leaf pondweed transported to Tahoe on contaminated boats quickly found refuge there.

Upper Truckee Marsh in 1940 shows where (dashed line) the Tahoe Keys subdivision was dredged into existence [40]. (*Google Earth*)

Upper Truckee Marsh in 2018 showing the Tahoe Keys development [40]. (*Google Earth*)

The dredging of the peninsulas destroyed prime nesting habitats for waterfowl. This loss of 500 acres of wetland alone accounted for 11 percent of the total loss of the naturally functioning wetlands at Tahoe that filtered out waterborne pollutants. All told, Tahoe Keys was an environmental disaster of monstrous proportions that appeared early in the resort development boom era and continues to be an open infected wound in Lake Tahoe's gut.

To meet the increased demand for goods and services from residents and visitors, growth in the private sector and infrastructure footprints on the land stayed in lockstep with the overall growth in these sectors. For the southern extent of the Tahoe Basin, private sector (commercial, industrial, and services) entities covered 69 acres in 1969. By 2002, their affected area was 621 acres, an eightfold increase over thirty-four years. In the same period, the supporting public infrastructure (transportation and utilities) footprint increased fourfold. Comparable figures are not available for the remainder of the affected Tahoe watershed, but qualitatively, similarly accelerated growth occurred. These commercial properties were sources of polluted runoff from the pavement, roofs, and walkways and erosion from bare soil.

As commercial and residential development increased, the use of automobiles increased dramatically. The exhaust of hundreds of thousands of vehicles contributed to air and water quality degradation in several ways. The Tahoe Basin's propensity is to develop an atmospheric inversion that traps these exhaust pollutants, worsening already adverse conditions.

For the entire basin, periods of non-attainment for ozone, carbon monoxide, particulate matter, and visibility often occurred between 1991–2011.

Tailpipe emissions of oxides of nitrogen settled out overnight and dissolved into the waters of Lake Tahoe. This dissolved nitrogen altered the lake's sensitive nutrient balance and stimulated the growth of water-clouding algae. The scarcity of dissolved nitrogen had

Summer traffic congestion in South Lake Tahoe [37]. (*Greg Johnson, bestlaketahoe.com*)

always limited Lake Tahoe's algal population. In-basin vehicle emissions and sources carried into the basin from outside the basin contributed to a surplus of dissolved nitrogen. The other essential nutrient for algae growth—phosphorus—was transported in stream flows from disturbed soils caused by land development.

In the early 1980s, the reversal to phosphorus control of algae growth was complete. The algae growth rate could increase because available dissolved nitrogen was no longer in short supply. A 2006 research study concluded 90 percent of the air deposition of nitrogen originated in the Tahoe Basin.

Abrasive sand grains applied to the roadways and parking lots to improve winter traction wore down into fine particles. These particles either washed off into the lake or became airborne and eventually settled into the lake. Fine particles are one of the two major causes of water clarity loss, the other being algae productivity.

At the dawn of the resort boom era of 1960–2000, the resident population was about 20,000 in 1960 and reached 56,000 in 2010. The peak population of permanent and seasonal residents, tourists, and day users shot up from 105,000 to 300,000. Housing units surged over forty years from 7,094 to an alarming 45,880. Two moderate-sized ski areas (Palisades Tahoe and Heavenly Valley) grew to well-known status. In concert, other key players (Sierra at Tahoe, Diamond Peak, Homewood, Alpine Meadows, Northstar, and Kirkwood) appeared in the region. There had been only a few small casinos. There were now four major casino hotels on the south end and two moderate-sized casino hotels on the north, in addition to many lodging and commercial properties.

The rise of gaming revenue on the South Shore was illustrative of the dramatic growth of the industry. Between 1960 and 2000, gaming revenues jumped from $25.7 million to $352.7 million, a whopping 1,272 percent increase. Annual average daily traffic, a measure of total vehicles in one location in both directions over a day, reached 398,00 vehicles in 2000, a 39 percent increase from 1974, the first year of such measurements.

At the close of the resort boom era in 2000, Tahoe was approaching full buildout. The feverish pace of new development began to taper off as the combination of scarce and high-priced vacant land, strict development regulations, and unfavorable economic conditions took hold. Skier days were leveling off at around 3.1 million per year. Annual visitation was 23 million, creating a $1.5 billion tourism-based economy that generated 36,000 jobs.

The harmful effects on the lake were a different story. Though sediment discharge varies widely year over year, the spot statistics were still alarming. In 1960, the total amount of sediment flowing into Lake Tahoe on an annual basis was 35.3 tons. By 2000, it had jumped to 90.4 tons, increasing 1.5 times the amount in 1960. Compare these to the undisturbed natural sediment discharge rate of 3.1 tons per year. The concentration of algae growing in the lake increased by a shocking 469 percent over the same period. Together, these two factors reduced the average clarity from 102.4 feet in 1968 to 67.4 feet in 2000.

As measured by observing the water depth at which and 10-inch white disk (Secchi disk) disappears, clarity had lost an average of about 1 foot per year for thirty-three years. The culprits were fine sediment and nutrient-driven algae growth. Fine sediments came from land disturbance and roadway abrasives, and nutrients occurred in runoff from impervious

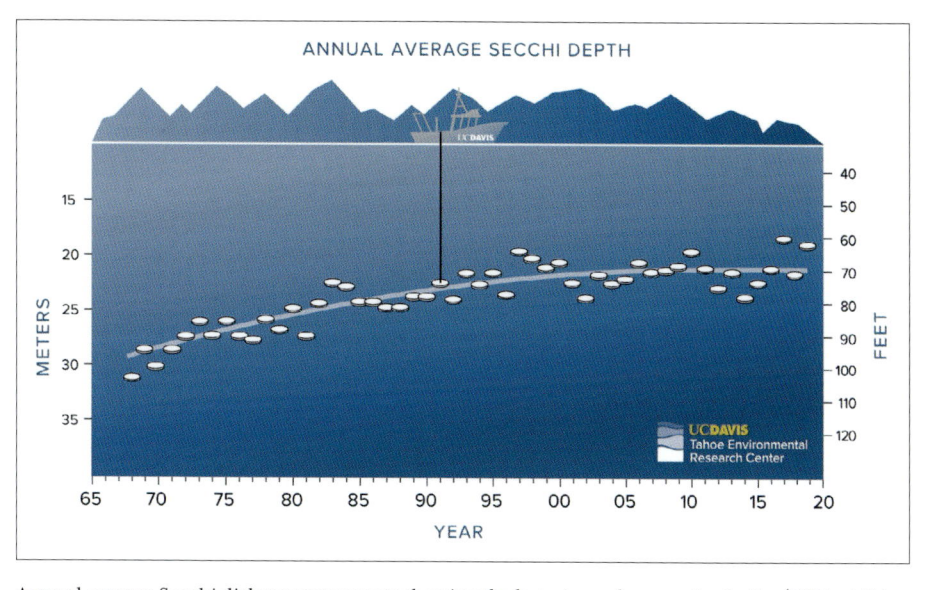

Annual average Secchi disk measurements showing the long-term decrease in clarity. (*UC Davis Tahoe Environmental Research Center*)

surfaces and automobile emissions. Undoubtedly, Lake Tahoe was in trouble and caught in a disastrous downward spiral.

Anecdotal evidence indicates that nuisance growths of algae on rocks and piers became commonly noticeable by the mid-1970s. Before that, lake scientist Charles R. Goldman saw an increase in attached algae growth by the mid-1960s compared to the late 1950s. Even Mark Twain recalled that submerged rocks were clean and their colors visible during his visits in 1861. The human-caused environmental changes preceding the 1970s potentially stimulated this condition before monitoring attached algae began in 1982.

Until 1975, there was declining widespread use of individual on-site waste disposal systems such as septic tanks. Also, several instances of in-basin disposal of treated sewage effluent from community systems occurred during this time. Researchers point to this period of in-basin wastewater disposal as the possible culprit. They suspect sewage discharges continued to taint the groundwater until all habitable structures were connected to the sewer, halting the pollution and creating a "pulse" of degraded groundwater moving slowly into the lake. A recent study showed the amount of attached algae biomass had trended downward since the onset of measurements in 1982. If a pulse of sewage tainted groundwater is the cause, this trend may indicate that the polluted mass is now in decline, as one might expect.

Lake Tahoe real estate has been a story of godforsaken land that gradually became valuable and in high demand. Lake Tahoe's land values stagnated following the logging era, with timber companies holding large tracts with no real value. In the 1930s, George Whittell, a reclusive multimillionaire, conducted sprawling land acquisitions totaling

45,000 acres encompassing more than 20 miles of shoreline. The sales prices varied from $3 to $6 per acre, depending on how close it was to the lake. These acquisitions covered all the Nevada shoreline and front country of the lake. The only exceptions were the Glenbrook and Stateline areas.

Throughout the 1940s and early 1950s, individual lots sold for a few hundred dollars, with lakefront lots going for as little as $1,000. By the 1970s, buildable residential lots varied from $3,000 to $10,000 depending on size, location, and view. Lakefront land sold for $1,000 per linear foot of waterfront.

In 1983, an Incline Village lakefront home sold for $1.35 million, marking the first time a sale exceeded the million-dollar residential price threshold at Tahoe. Since then, and except for brief periods of economic weakness, prices have skyrocketed. The owner of a lakefront luxury mansion on Crystal Bay listed their property for $75 million in 2018.

In 2019, large lakefront homes' sales typically ranged into the $10–20 million segments, while modern lake view homes hover around $2-3 million. Over the twenty-four years ending in April 2020, the Tahoe housing market in Placer County increased at the average rate of 9.8 percent per year.

Historically, the resort development boom era was the time of most environmental harm to the lake and its watershed by the persistence of impacts and their degree of irreversibility.

Surely the resource exploitation era exacted a sizeable toll on the lake and its watershed. The nature of the watershed destruction was severe but not an irreversible change. However, unlike the resort development boom, the post-resource exploitation ecological communities of the lake and watershed had time to partially recover and begin moving back toward a natural condition unless impeded by human intervention.

Human-built changes in the resort development boom era were far more resistant to a natural recovery and progression back to an undisturbed condition. Buildings and roads are highly resilient to the effects of age and decomposition. In comparison, nineteenth-century deforestation left few durable structures and artifacts. Reversing the impacts of the resort development boom era requires a considerable input of funds and human effort. As we will see in the following chapters, the cost and effort to remove physical objects, undo ecological modifications, and implement long-term restoration is substantial. Equally challenging is mitigating the effects of the built public and private infrastructure that remains.

There was no doubt that Tahoe was a highly desirable location for recreation and real estate investment in this era. The cost to the environment was substantial and threatened the very reasons people sought Tahoe as a destination. Rapidly declining water clarity, degraded scenic vistas, traffic jams, and polluted air were on one side of the scale. On the other side was the potential to profit, make a living, and own a piece of paradise. With one side propelled by money objectives and the other side fueled with a protectionist passion, conditions simmered for the coming highly emotional political and legal warfare over the Tahoe Basin's future.

9

Environmental Conflict, Reconciliation, and Collaboration (1970–2000)

It is helpful to review the actions and conflicts in the decades preceding this era. The Tahoe Conflict over private use instead of preserving it for public benefit was an ongoing theme that arose with the Tahoe Basin's permanent occupation by profit-minded Euro-Americans. The earliest struggles involved nineteenth-century forest practices by timber companies. Critics sought government protection with no success. The forced relocation of the Washoe tribe and suppressing their ways elicited strong but futile protests by tribal members.

Water diversions from the Truckee River began in the 1860s but depended solely on the run of the river flows from its uncontrolled tributaries and outflow from Lake Tahoe. There was no meaningful year-over-year storage to even out wet and dry years and extend the irrigation season. Water users were wholly reliant on that year's amount of winter precipitation. If snowfall was sparse, the river's resulting runoff was equally meager in volume and the amount of time water flowed.

Just after the turn of the twentieth century, government water planners and Nevada development interests turned their eyes to Tahoe's abundant waters. Proposals for constructing a Tahoe dam, lowering the lake's outlet rim, and a future water diversion tunnel into the Washoe Valley provoked opposition from shoreline property owners. Harm to valuable waterfront land due to unprecedented extremes in water level and flooding and high-water erosion, and lost use of their piers were real dangers. The Lake Tahoe Protective Association, the first organized advocacy group for Tahoe, opposed these and other environmentally harmful actions. Acting as a group and as individuals, they successfully obtained reasonable lake levels by preventing the lowering of the natural rim, limiting the highest lake level, and halting work toward an export tunnel. Policies such as the Truckee River Agreement of 1935 set an upper limit on the elevation of stored water at 6,229.1 feet Lake Tahoe datum (LTD). LTD is an abbreviation to the archaic reference to historical sea level that is unique to Lake Tahoe. LTD is 1.14 feet below currently recognized sea level elevation.

Following the short skirmish over water resources and the rest of the first half of the twentieth century, relative calm prevailed as Tahoe marked time through the Great Depression and World War II. However, tempers began to flare again, this time over land use and growth in the post-war era of prosperity and population growth.

The earliest sign of conflict between citizens and land developers with their allied commercial interests appeared in 1957 with the Tahoe Improvement and Conservation Association formation. Alarmed by rapidly accelerating urbanization, wealthy second homeowners raised funds and hired staff and attorneys to influence future planning. It would be the opening shot in a decades-long struggle over the future of Lake Tahoe.

In 1959 and response to the environmentally destructive Tahoe Keys project, environmental, commercial, and land developer interests came together to form the Lake Tahoe Area Council. The nonprofit organization would serve as a vehicle for the parties to create and work toward a shared vision. The faulty underlying assumption was that all parties agreed growth and economic expansion would continue but only occur under an umbrella of planning guidelines.

In 1963, the council produced a comprehensive report on Lake Tahoe that called for universal sewering of all habitable structures and the export of treated wastewater from the Lake Tahoe watershed. Parallel export of all refuse was another recommendation. The council's engineering consultants decided the ecologically sensitive lake required a ban on all waste discharges within the watershed. However, the report omitted a troubling implication—the design of the wastewater systems would serve a massive amount of growth based on buildout to the full potential of very liberal local zoning. In 1974, this became a highly inflamed point of conflict.

The report overlooked the unrealized water quality impacts of land development on soil erosion, stormwater runoff, and automotive emissions that growth would bring. It would not be until the following years of scientific study that scientists and planners would understand these effects.

As a second strategy, the council fostered the Tahoe Regional Planning Commission's creation, an advisory body composed of various governments around the lake. At this point and with a few exceptions, the competing interests of protectionism and pro-development agreed on the priority actions of sewering and wastewater export with no apparent disputes over the continued residential and commercial urbanization of the Tahoe Basin, each having in mind a much different outcome.

The Tahoe Regional Planning Commission produced a 1980 regional plan in 1964 that painted a grandiose picture of an urbanized Tahoe. The plan alarmed many with its scenario of three roadway belts composed of a freeway, parkway, and local road ringing the lake. It included a much-despised proposal for a bridge over the mouth of Emerald Bay.

The roadways would serve an average population of 313,000 persons and a peak of 600,000 persons based on full buildout to generous local zoning limits. The plan's narrative explained that its vision was "based on the political premise that building a strongly interlinked economy was the most desirable future outcome for the region." Remarkably absent was any mention of the welfare of the lake.

Tahoe Regional Planning Commission Plan prepared in 1964 for 1980. (*League to Save Lake Tahoe*)

Governors Ronald Reagan and Paul Laxalt at Heavenly Valley Ski Area [34] in 1967 to conduct negotiations over the Tahoe Regional Planning Compact. (*Don Dondero, University of Nevada, Special Collections*)

The 1980 regional plan advanced the private use priority over public benefit in the Tahoe Conflict debate. The reaction was swift and furious. The newly renamed League to Save Lake Tahoe, formerly the Tahoe Improvement and Conservation Association, slammed the plan publicly and stepped up their lobbying efforts to bring sensible planning and growth limits to the basin.

The two states created a Lake Tahoe Joint Study Commission in 1965. The commission held public meetings and issued its report in 1967. The report recommended creating a regional planning agency with authority over land use and overseen by a governing board of at-large and local representatives. In response, the two states negotiated a bistate compact with each state approving the proposed legislation followed by congressional ratification and the president's signature. Article 1, Section 10, Clause 3 of the U.S. Constitution permits two or more states to enter into agreements or compacts only with Congress's consent.

The bistate Tahoe Regional Planning Agency (TRPA) became active in 1970 under the Tahoe Regional Planning Compact ratified the previous year. The agency held authority over nearly every aspect of human activity that could affect the lake or its watershed in California and Nevada. Improbably, Coe Swobe, a Nevada elected official passionate about Lake Tahoe, brokered the deal.

Understandably, each state was concerned about the other state dictating to it. The fear of losing a state's rights to another state or, worse, governance by a non-elected bureaucratic agency was the driving force that forged a less than perfect solution.

To the dismay of environmentalists, the heavily compromised compact harbored three fatal flaws. Added by Nevada, (1) a "dual majority" rule mandated a majority vote of both state's delegations for a project's denial, (2) a "60-day" rule granted automatic approval to any project not denied by a dual majority vote within the 60 days, and added by California, (3) a governing board composed of a majority of development-friendly local officials in each state's delegation rather than a balance with the at-large representatives. These flaws gave just three members of one state's panel the power to withhold a dual majority denial, causing a project to receive default approval after sixty days of inaction.

Beginning at its start in 1970, the TRPA struggled with the creation of a regional plan. The first plan, which proposed strict growth limits, failed, and its mastermind, Executive Director J. K. Smith, resigned.

A second plan, designed by politically astute local government planning official Richard Heikka, was more palatable, even as it downzoned thousands of raw land acres. An innovative element of the plan was incorporating a land capability system that dictated limits on the amount of impervious coverage (pavement and structures) a site could handle. Allowed impervious coverage varied from 1 percent for the most sensitive wetlands and steep erodible slopes to 30 percent for the most suitable flat land with permeable soil. The result was to slash in half the original projected peak day population of 600,000 tourists and residents by 2010. Known informally by its pragmatic progenitor's name, the "Heikka Plan" contained no restrictions on the rates or types of growth that could occur.

Over 1970–71, TRPA approved 99 percent of the projects presented to it. In 1973, Harvey's Wagon Wheel expansion, Raley's North Shore Mall, and three new casino hotels—Park Tahoe, Tahoe Palace, and Hotel Oliver—gained sixty-day default approval. In the ensuing years, traffic-increasing multilevel parking garages for South Shore casino hotels and a loop road around its casino core to serve the garages cleared TRPA review.

Much litigation ensued, led by the League to Save Lake Tahoe, Sierra Club, Natural Resources Defense Council, and the California Attorney General. Many of these cases landed in Reno's Federal Court, where a provincial interest found little sympathy for the plaintiffs.

Environmentalists and old-time Tahoe preservationists were incredulous and issued calls for more action and reform of TRPA. In response, California did what it could in 1974 by strengthening the California Tahoe Regional Planning Agency (CTRPA), but it only had authority over the California side.

CTRPA took a strict environmental protectionist approach. It banned new subdivisions and condominiums, prohibited all development on sensitive lands, and approved a transportation plan that emphasized transit systems over the automobile. Its innovative transportation plan proposed building intercept parking lots in Myers and Truckee and encouraged incoming tourists to use transit buses.

Planners reasoned that controlling the highways on the California side could stem the congested traffic flow into the Tahoe Basin in general and specifically to the South Shore casinos. However, it never achieved this goal. At least in California, the Tahoe Conflict debate had migrated back to the public benefit side even if the results were not impressive.

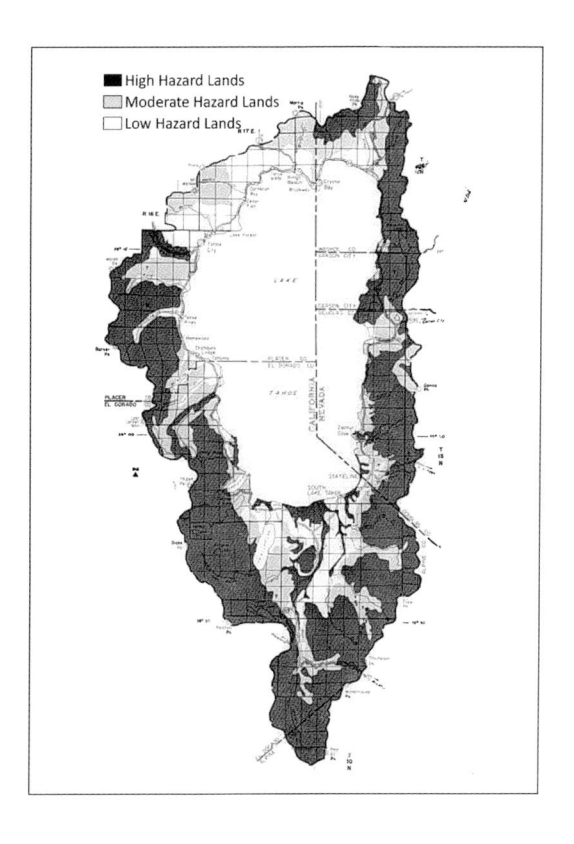

Bailey land hazard map, an early
(1971) attempt to map the extent of
environmentally sensitive lands.
(*Modified from Robert G. Bailey*)

This time the blowback was from local development interests and local governments
who joined forces to engage in an opposition strategy of protest, civil disobedience, and
confrontation. Local leaders became incensed that the CTRPA board (composed of a voting
majority of out-of-the-area political appointees) eclipsed land-use decisions made by
local elected officials. A second rallying cry was opposition to enacting a moratorium on
developing ecologically sensitive lands. They asserted this was an unconstitutional taking
of private property rights.

In 1974, Roy C. Hampson, the mercurial executive officer of the Lahontan Water Board,
ordered his staff to take a closer look at wastewater treatment and export capabilities on the
California side. By May 1975, following a wet winter and rapid snowmelt, the interim treated
wastewater disposal system serving the north and west shores in California overflowed
into the Truckee River. The result was a sewer connection ban that brought a temporary
halt to the uncontrolled building boom for second homes. The South Shore followed in
1977 when its highly touted advanced wastewater treatment and disposal system failed
to meet water quality standards. Again, the Water Board imposed a connection ban and
offered grant funds to solve the problem.

On the Nevada side near Stateline, the treatment plant serving the casino core and
residential areas from Glenbrook and southward failed to meet discharge standards.

Benign neglect by the Nevada Department of Environmental Protection opened the door to an attempted injunction on new connections sought by the Natural Resources Defense Council and Sierra Club with technical assistance from California. Since the trial occurred in a Nevada-based federal court, the only result was a consent decree that temporarily slowed the rate of new connections and obligated the sewer district to do what it was already mandated to do. Nevada-based Federal Judge Harry Claiborne declared the environment "must give way" for human progress to occur during the hearing on the injunction.

As tension over more land-use restrictions and outright moratoria heightened, advocacy groups such as the Council for Logic formed and mounted an all-out battle with lake scientists and regulators. Council for Logic representatives instigated one of the earliest attacks on science-based environmental decision-making by characterizing basic research into the lake as "pseudo-science." They argued that since the air and water pollution of the nineteenth-century logging era was worse than the current situation and the lake water quality still recovered, it somehow justified continued environmental degradation in the watershed. Presaging the current crop of climate change deniers, they questioned whether humans caused the lake's changes and suggested it was all part of a natural cycle.

The single-family dwelling construction boom of the 1970s had spawned a real estate and construction industry composed of small businesses wholly dependent upon profits from these units' sales. As regulatory and planning agencies tightened building restrictions, lot owners became more fearful of losing their investment. The anxiety stimulated an acceleration in building permits as owners tried to get in "under the wire" with such tactics as building only a foundation to lock in their development rights.

The rapidly increasing demand spurred more slow-growth policies and restrictions. This response, in turn, raised the heat on justifiably fearful owners. The result was a perpetual motion machine of increasing growth pressures driven by fear on both sides. The disruption in this harmful cycle did not occur until the Lahontan Water Board-imposed sewer connection moratoria mentioned earlier. By 1980, a revitalized TRPA was able to oversee growth management.

Turmoil roiled public meetings. One such incident in 1977 occurred when a contractor marched in the center aisle of a public meeting room, ranting for a violent overthrow of the CTRPA. Armed police officers often stood in the back of the room at board meetings and controversial public hearings while patrol cars circled the meeting locations. These emotional flare-ups were not unexpected; the new rules would wipe out or severely cut back livelihoods and threaten working families' economic stability.

Rumors of hired killers circulated, and enraged locals threatened and harassed public agency staff members with face-to-face confrontations and middle-of-the-night nuisance phone calls. Public agency employees Mike James and Steve Chilton were victims of violent assaults while performing their official inspection duties.

In defiance of stop-work orders and as a protest, contractor Robert Pershing built an entire home on sensitive land without a CTRPA permit, becoming one of many who "bootlegged" their construction projects. Builders reasoned the end justified the means; since

Aerial view of Pomin Park. In the image center, the large flat area was the 1980 unpermitted playing field construction site within environmentally sensitive lands [41]. In 2021, several agencies were studying the feasibility of site restoration. (*Salix Consulting*)

the restrictions were unconstitutional in their view, they were justified in proceeding without legally required approvals.

Towards the end of the protest and civil disobedience phase, in 1980, a group of contractors, construction workers, and youth athletic volunteers mounted an unlawful effort to construct a playing field on impacted sensitive wetlands in Lake Forest [41]. The group was frustrated with several project approval delays and wanted to provide an athletic field for community youth.

For its part, Nevada remained critical and obstinate toward the effort to repair environmental damage if it meant less growth. In one meeting about an environmental impact report for an upgrade to a California wastewater treatment plant, a California representative proposed considering a rollback of undesirable development as a form of mitigation for the new growth the upgrade would allow. The Nevada Department of Environmental Protection administrator bristled at the idea and labeled it "asinine." Of course, more progressive leaders from both states at TRPA embraced the "rollback as offset" concept in later years. Nevada would eventually come around beginning in 1983 with a twenty-four-year string of three enlightened governors of both parties who took an active role in leading the Nevada administrative state to a supportive position. The trend continues today after a lone setback in 2007–2011.

The tense times showed the best and worst in people. Terry Trupp, who served as executive director of the Council for Logic and mayor of South Lake Tahoe, faced a money laundering conviction. The chairman of the CTRPA, Tahoe City realtor Gordon Hooper, dealt with a particularly challenging situation that found him courageously voting in the lake's best interests. He then endured harsh treatment and social ostracization in his hometown of Tahoe City for his principled stands.

The California-only CTRPA proposals to restrict growth pressured Nevada to engage in lengthy negotiations to resolve differences and forge a revised bistate Tahoe Regional Planning Compact. Led by state senator and rancher John Garamendi of California and Nevada assemblymember and casino owner Joe Dini, they reached an agreement in 1979.

The revised compact gave birth to a reinvented TRPA that regained control in 1980. It fixed the inherent flaws of its previous incarnation, enacted a prohibition on new casino hotels, and mandated environmental threshold carrying capacity benchmarks. The "thresholds" would serve as standards for the measurement of TRPA effectiveness. In 1981, TRPA ordered a moratorium on new housing until a regional plan became a reality. As part of the bistate deal, the California-only CTRPA, intensely despised by Nevada and local government officials in California, phased out in 1982.

The revised compact touched off more conflict and litigation. Sophisticated and more professional pro-property rights groups emerged and entered the fray—the Tahoe-Sierra Preservation Council and the South Tahoe Gaming Alliance. The League to Save Lake Tahoe and the Sierra Club, both environmental advocacy groups, became more entrenched. All sides opened new litigation fronts. Environmentalists successfully sued to halt the regional plan and achieved a court-supervised moratorium that depressed the construction economy.

The central figure for the Tahoe-Sierra Preservation Council was its general counsel, Tahoe City attorney Larry Hoffman. Hoffman was known as an articulate and formidable adversary who possessed strong powers of persuasion. Earlier in his career, he successfully argued self-defense in a coroner's inquest into a Los Angeles police officer's six-shot killing of a drugged and naked, unarmed man.

Hoffman assumed a more civil, logical, and constructive stance than his predecessors. He and his property rights allies sought compensation for loss of use of land due to an alleged unconstitutional taking of private property rights. The Fifth Amendment to the U.S. Constitution prohibits the government from executing a unilateral taking of personal property rights without compensating the owner. In this case, the proponents argued the government took away the right to build without just payment. Meanwhile, the property rights advocates negotiated with TRPA and other agencies to obtain movement toward their respective points of view. In an act of buyer's remorse in 1984, Nevada made threats to withdraw from the compact if changes in how TRPA respected property rights did not occur.

Though the situation seemed hopeless, some progress occurred outside of the TRPA battlefield. Local governments achieved the sewering and export of all wastewater in 1975. The federal Santini-Burton Act of 1980 made funds available to buy vacant lands deprived of development potential and provided local governments money for erosion control projects. California followed this with its own $85 million land purchase bond in 1982 and activated the California Tahoe Conservancy land acquisition program. These actions began to quell the anger over perceived unconstitutional takings of private property rights.

With the land-use planning and approval process at loggerheads in 1985, Bill Morgan, the new executive director of TRPA, floated the concept of a broad consensus-building process involving all stakeholders. Morgan, a career Forest Service engineer and manager, was familiar with the successes of this process in resolving forest management disputes.

Morgan brought together these six categories of stakeholders: federal agencies and tribal governments, California state agencies and local governments, Nevada state agencies and local governments, scientific research institutions, environmental and property rights advocacy groups, and TRPA itself as the instrument of plan implementation.

Consensus building brings warring parties to the table and, using a neutral facilitator, incrementally builds up "consensus" over solutions to contentious issues. Over several years of meetings, former adversaries negotiated over their differences, found common ground, and injected their joint solutions into a new regional plan.

The consensus process broke the deadlock by creating an innovative system to evaluate land development potential and priority using scoring systems and a program that would allow the transfer or sale of private property development rights. Every individual subdivision lot now had a chance to develop in the future and recover lost value through other means. Other aspects included a procedure for each community to establish its plan within the more extensive regional plan framework, a ban on new development on sensitive lands, limits on commercial expansion, and a continued ban on new land subdivisions, including condominiums.

The 1987 regional plan received TRPA governing board approval, and the plan and implementing ordinances became effective July 1, 1987. The two states and the Forest Service cranked up their land acquisition programs, which afforded two benefits. Low-scoring landholders now had an opportunity to recover their investment by selling immediately instead of waiting decades for their chance to arrive. Secondly, aggressive acquisition policies aimed toward willing sellers permanently removed environmentally sensitive low-scoring lands from development potential.

During the consensus-building process of 1985–1987, a long-simmering struggle over public access to beaches on the California side effectively ended. In 1977, the California State Lands Commission asserted state ownership and control of the shore zone below the high-water mark of lakes and rivers. The state received title to these lands upon its admission to the Union in 1850. In 1872, the legislature granted title to these lands between the high-water and low-water marks to adjacent (littoral) property owners. This act set the stage for disagreement over the right of public access to these lands after the legislature's 1872 action.

At Tahoe and elsewhere throughout the state, litigation ensued over the years to resolve the question. In 1986, the California Appellant Court of the Third Appellant District ruled on a Tahoe-specific case. When the legislature granted title to littoral owners, the court held that it did not give up its public trust interest in the subject lands. The state of California has the public trust interest for the benefit of the public for purposes of commerce, navigation, fishing, recreation, and preservation of the land in its natural state.

South Upper Truckee River Marsh is an example of environmentally sensitive land that the 1987 Regional Plan protected. (*jcookfisher, Creative Commons*)

The Appellant Court ruling meant the public could access and use the lake bottom between the low-water and high-water marks under conditions like those granted by an easement. An easement gives privileges of access and use to private lands but not ownership rights.

After investigation, the court determined the low-water mark was 6,223 feet LTD, the natural rim of Lake Tahoe. However, the court rejected the previously agreed maximum water level of 6,229.1 feet LTD for storage as the high-water mark. Instead, it pointed to the calculated natural average high-water level of 6,228.75 feet LTD as the historical high-water mark. While the difference is almost negligible, it opened Tahoe's beaches in California to public access for recreation, fishing, and navigation. In practice, the public could now pass over and temporarily occupy land below the high-water mark in front of private property, subject to the law and local ordinances. In Nevada, littoral private property rights extend to the low-water mark with no public trust access for now.

Following the successful outcome of the consensus-building process, residual tensions remained. Nevertheless, formerly contentious stakeholders did not forget the lessons of collaborative problem-solving. Realizing actual accomplishments could occur within agreement areas, interest group leaders organized the Lake Tahoe Transportation and Water Quality Coalition (TTWQ Coalition) in 1989. Steve Teshara of the pro-property rights Tahoe-Sierra Preservation Council and the Rochelle Nason of the environmentalist League to Save Lake Tahoe co-chaired the group. The eighteen-member TTWQ Coalition included environmental groups, public agencies, property rights advocates, gaming interests, large businesses, business organizations, and TRPA. Its overarching goal was to forge partnerships for Lake Tahoe's benefit by solving existing environmental problems in agreement areas among the parties. Notably, this marked the beginning of private business interests taking a more active and direct role in shaping the future of environmental improvement in the Tahoe Basin through closer interaction with oversight agencies.

In February 1997, the ghosts of old animosities arose and regressed to violence. TRPA had denied tour boat operator Joe Thiemann a permit to relocate and continue his business. Probably recognizing this as the total loss of his livelihood, Thiemann resorted to violence. He was shot to death at the house of the owner of his former port as he tried to exact revenge for the eviction. Officials discovered Thiemann's vehicle with weapons, and many speculate his next stop was the TRPA governing board meeting that was still in session. Years earlier, authorities implicated Thiemann in an assault on a TRPA inspector monitoring Thiemann's tour boat operation for permit compliance.

Public agencies tightened security, including installing a "panic button" for the TRPA governing board. The thought of mass casualties was a sobering image that caused all sides to turn down the temperature of political rhetoric.

In July 1997, the TTWQ Coalition's efforts reached one of many high-water marks by hosting the inaugural Lake Tahoe Presidential Forum attended by President Bill Clinton and Vice-President Al Gore. In a week of meetings and appearances, high-ranking federal and state officials discussed challenges and aired solutions.

President Clinton observed at the forum, "The model of cooperation you have established will be a model we will want to use across the country." Vice-President Gore added, "Lake Tahoe demonstrates that the environment is the economy and the economy is the environment."

Lake scientist Charles R. Goldman hosted Clinton and Gore on his research vessel, measuring water clarity. The event would become an annual occurrence hosted alternately by California's and Nevada's senators.

In the ensuing years, Former President Bill Clinton returned on the forum's tenth anniversary in 2006. President Barack Obama made his first visit to Tahoe in 2016 to commemorate the two decades of joint progress toward environmental protection.

One year after the first presidential forum of 1997, TRPA released an ambitious $1 billion list of private and public projects to achieve the regional plan's goals and thresholds. That same year, Congress approved the Southern Nevada Public Lands Management Act (SNPLMA). Under SNPLMA, the Bureau of Land Management sold surplus federal lands surrounding then-burgeoning Las Vegas. The sales proceeds became available in 2003 to fund Tahoe environmental improvements such as sensitive land acquisition, ecological research, water, air, habitat, and transportation improvement projects.

In the nation's capital in 2000, California and Nevada U.S. Senators Dianne Feinstein (D-CA) and Harry Reid (D-NV) introduced the $300 million Lake Tahoe Restoration Act. This legislation became the first of many such bills and fulfilled the funding pledge made by President Clinton in 1997.

The final gasp of the pro-property rights movement occurred in 2002 when the U.S. Supreme Court upheld the ability of TRPA to restrict the use of private land as a regulatory

President Bill Clinton aboard the Research Vessel *John Le Conte* views zooplankton through a magnification lens as Vice-president Al Gore (left) and Dr. Charles Goldman look on. (*UC Davis, Tahoe Environmental Research Center*)

action affecting private property rights and was not an act of taking without just compensation. In a twist of national significance, U.S. Justice Department Attorney John Roberts successfully represented TRPA—the same John Roberts who ascended to the U.S. Supreme Court as chief justice in 2005.

Since the U.S. Supreme Court decision, the property rights movement has gone chiefly silent except for a few groups that engage in very narrowly defined property interests, such as lakefront properties and commercial marinas. Even these groups eschew a combative approach, choosing instead to work collaboratively with TRPA and other agencies. In response, land-use and regulatory agencies abandoned their top-down "command and control" regulatory model. They moved toward an ongoing collaborative approach with broader and deeper involvement and influence by stakeholders.

Prospective water users with grandiose plans mentioned earlier in this chapter have long eyed the Truckee River and Lake Tahoe. The lengthy history of conflict, threats of violence, negotiations, litigation, and legislation ranks among the most protracted interstate water rights disputes in U.S. history. It is far too complex to explain here except to hit the critical points related to Lake Tahoe.

As one venerable water rights attorney summed it up, the federal government repeatedly gave away the same water without regard to pre-existing users' rights. Water rights were implicitly reserved by the predecessor to the Bureau of Indian Affairs when it created the Pyramid Lake Paiute Reservation in 1859. The future set-aside provided sufficient water rights to sustain the lake and its fisheries upon which the tribe depended. In 1902, the Bureau of Reclamation appropriated much of the Truckee River flow for the Newlands Irrigation Project. Add to this demand the water use by agriculture in the Truckee Meadows, Reno and Sparks' urban areas, and residential and commercial users in the California portion of the watershed.

Decades of negotiations over an interstate water compact failed to achieve congressional ratification because it lacked an acceptable solution to the loss of water inflow into Pyramid Lake. The upstream diversions resulted in an 84-foot decline in lake level and severely damaged fisheries. For several complex legal and statutory reasons, the Pyramid Lake Paiutes' rights were superior to all others.

Nevada U.S. Senator Harry Reid saw the need to bring the parties to the negotiating table to reach an agreement embodied in federal law. The result was the Truckee-Carson-Pyramid Lake Water Rights Settlement Act of 1990. The Truckee River Operating Agreement, approved in 2008, promulgates the implementing rules.

The law allocated the water between the states and among the primary users. The Tahoe Basin received an annual allocation of 23,000 acre-feet for the California side and 11,000 acre-feet for Nevada side. A court-appointed watermaster oversees mandated water rights for tribal, fish, wildlife, agricultural, and municipal uses. Oddly, 95 percent of the water originates as runoff in California, but 95 percent of the permitted use under the 1990 act occurs in Nevada.

This settlement's environmental consequences mean protecting endangered fish species and stable reservoir levels to support fish, wildlife, and recreation. The benefits are more efficient water use, better water supply management, and assured hydropower generation flows. On the legal front, it ordered the dismissal of all pending litigation that threatened the loss of critical water rights of existing users and confirmed the interstate allocations of water.

As the curtain fell on this era in 2002, Lake Tahoe still faced many serious hurdles resulting from decades of abuse, benign neglect, and dysfunctional governance complicated by more recent changes in the global climate. The 2001 environmental thresholds evaluation revealed an alarming 70 percent of the original 1997 thresholds were not in the attainment status.

For its part, the once litigious League to Save Lake Tahoe scaled back its aggressive watchdog role. Under the new executive leadership of Darcie Goodman Collins, they initiated hands-on preservation and restoration programs at the grassroots level. Notable examples are forest stewardship days, citizen observation and reporting on aquatic ecology, and monitoring stormwater pipe discharges. The Tahoe Sierra Preservation Council and South Tahoe Gaming Alliance both went dormant.

Basin actors can look back on this era as an unpleasant but closed chapter in Tahoe's environmental protection history. Perhaps it was a cultural evolution process that the region had to pass through before accepting the reality of Lake Tahoe's imposed vision and the limitations on achieving that vision.

The growing pains produced a better climate of mutual trust, collaboration, and civil behavior to carry out the process of protecting and restoring the Tahoe Basin. Reaching maturity in environmental governance involves accepting that individual interest is subordinate to a greater public good while respecting personal views and constitutional rights. Add to these the necessity of local economic viability where possible and acknowledge the responsibility to future generations. One might say this was the logical and most desirable outcome of the Tahoe Conflict.

The fragile detente placed the lake's well-being and the region's economic health as mutually compatible goals, reinforced by continued good-faith actions by all sides. Referring to the "Tragedy of the Commons" analogy, shepherds could now add another animal to their flocks. However, they still must negotiate to remove stock animals from another's herd to ensure no overgrazing occurs and invest in the commons' overall health, leaving it as good as they found it. In the real world, this analogy means that new developments conform to modern standards on their building site, making them environmentally neutral. Also, they must offset some environmental impacts elsewhere and contribute to funds that support broader improvement projects such as regional transit systems. The net result is a steady rollback of past environmental wrongs and movement toward a sustainable future.

10

RESTORATION AND
REDEVELOPMENT
(2003–PRESENT)

Shortly after the dawn of the twenty-first century, the gradual change in land-use planning and philosophy by TRPA began to take hold. The systematic comparison of measured progress to the environmental threshold carrying capacity standards showed that direct regulation of land use was not as effective as it once was compared to an ecological restoration strategy. Indeed, by then, most of the Tahoe Basin approached buildout with little opportunity to urbanize vacant land, though TRPA still closely scrutinized new projects. TRPA faced a massive amount of pre-existing development that was a constant and significant source of pollution and needed comprehensive remediation to improve the lake's health.

The Tahoe tourism industry had reached its plateau of maturity in the late twentieth century and went through a self-examination period in the years that followed. The sector faced a choice to reshape its destiny or perish on the tourism battleground at the hands of more competitive all-service, all-season destination resorts such as Indian casinos and cheaply accessible Intermountain Region ski areas in Colorado, Utah, and Idaho. The casino competitors were closer to the urban centers than the Tahoe gaming customer base. The competitive advantage of Tahoe tourism was the lake, the uniqueness of its surrounding natural environment, and the quality of its lodging and outdoor tourism infrastructure. A meme for the time could have been, "It's the Lake, stupid!"

The Tahoe social environment was ripe for a newer and more enlightened approach. The entrenched tradition-oriented conservative generation of leaders released its grasp on power to a younger and progressive thinking group. The large-scale bitter growth battles were over. All parties understood the urgent need to conduct environmental restoration and redevelopment projects to restore the lake and its watershed. The ailing tourism industry was anxious to improve its infrastructure, modernize, and shift to meet the rapidly changing tourism market demands.

Continuing with their newfound policy-making approach of collaboration and broader participation, TRPA created closer ties with those needed to implement the agency's

ambitious goals. The agency backed away from top-down rulemaking and tight regulation. TRPA implemented a more extensive delegation of land-use regulation authority
and project inspection to local governments, made possible by the latter's abandonment
of their aggressive protest-oriented opposition strategy. TRPA executed memoranda of
understanding with state agencies that granted wider latitude for project approval and
ended duplicative regulation.

TRPA released its first comprehensive Environmental Improvement Plan (EIP) following
the presidential forum of 1997. Packed with over 1 billion dollars in environmental improvement projects needed to reverse Lake Tahoe's ecological and economic decline, funding the
EIP was a formidable challenge. Outside sources such as income from the federal government's Las Vegas land sale program (SNPLMA) and the Lake Tahoe Restoration Act offered
significant funding. Still, there was a deficit, and a local contribution seemed in order.

TRPA has long collected fees from new projects to fund its operations. Planners now
turned their attention to redevelopment projects as a funding source. TRPA levied hefty
mitigation fees on new projects, then redirected the payments to restoration and transportation improvement projects. These actions occurred in addition to making every project
mitigate and offset its impacts at a ratio greater than 1:1. Critics charged that this seemingly
perpetual cash machine would embed in the TRPA a bias toward project approvals.

The principle of using new projects to reduce net overall environmental impacts was not
new but gaining renewed interest. Previously in 2000, a proof-of-concept redevelopment
of the dilapidated South Lake Tahoe motel and commercial core occurred. A new gondola
serving the Heavenly Mountain Resort allowed skiers direct access on foot from new mixed-
use lodging and commercial areas. The new project removed more tourist hotel rooms
than it created and reduced traffic congestion by placing skiers within walking distance
of the ski area gondola.

Environmental improvement projects fell into three categories: restoration of the natural
environment, redevelopment of existing infrastructure, and transportation enhancements.
Over fifteen years ending in 2012, eight more significant streams and wet meadows had
restoration measures applied. Local governments added two major bike trails, and a new
transit center in Tahoe City began operation. In 2006, the UC Davis Tahoe Environmental
Research Center opened on Sierra Nevada University's campus [39]. A new visitor education
center opened at Sand Harbor State Park [42].

Putting its collaboration and participation principles to a real-world test, TRPA started a
years-long update to its 1987 regional plan in 2005. Christened Pathway 2007, the process
organized a forum for state agencies to make their respective resource management
plans consistent with the updated regional plan and develop recommended changes
to the existing regional plan. A series of public workshops and working groups would
gather feedback and develop specific recommendations. Their first product would be a
shared vision of the Tahoe region in the year 2027. The TRPA governing board approved
the highly idealized and aspirational vision statement in 2007. Intense work then began
rewriting the regional plan while sharing the work in progress with all stakeholders for
review and response.

Park Avenue and U.S. 50 Redevelopment Project before (right) and after (below) [34]. (*Design Workshop*)

Restored environmentally sensitive land before (left) and after. (*Tahoe Regional Planning Agency*)

Tahoe City Transit Center [25]. (*Placer County*)

The regional plan update received final approval in December 2012 and marked nothing less than a significant course correction in how the TRPA approached land use. The plan solved many issues related to streamlining, simplifying, and lowering barriers in the labyrinth of TRPA ordinances that governed most facets of physical human impact on the Tahoe Basin. For the first time, the concept of sustainability became an official touchstone for all future land-use decisions. Environmental sustainability is a concept that relies on the continued operation of a project by not depleting natural resources or creating irreversible impacts. Ironically, it was a throwback to the Washoe tribal philosophy of living in long-term balance with nature.

During the regional plan update process and after four years of exhaustive studies, hearings, and controversies, TRPA approved the Tahoe Beach Club in 2008. The project removed a dilapidated Stateline, Nevada, trailer park with lakefront access and replaced it with 143 luxury residences spread over 20 acres. The key elements that gained TRPA support consisted of major environmental restoration at the site and fifty-four units of achievable housing to replace the units displaced by removing the trailer park. Again, the concept of using new projects to correct the sins of the past found acceptance.

Given its newly found collaborative philosophy, TRPA in 2009 turned to its legal counsel, Joanne Marchetta, for its next executive director. She embedded into the regional plan the proven strategy of coupling new projects with onsite remediation and restoration elsewhere. Her approach was to leverage part of the incoming investment for innovative projects into funding for extensive on-site remediation and off-site restoration programs that would result in a net environmental benefit. It embodied a simple adage, "The project is the fix."

The new projects as solutions for old problems relied on a robust local economy flourishing in harmony with the environment. A stable, sustainable economy would provide project opportunities and initiatives to generate partial funding for remediation programs. TRPA and a consortium of local governments in the broader Lake Tahoe and Northern Nevada region founded the non-profit Tahoe Prosperity Center to bolster this approach. The center acts as an innovator and coordinator to "promote regional sustainability through economic vitality, environmental stewardship and healthy communities in and around the Lake Tahoe Basin."

The regional plan's central piece was a new strategy to create town centers of mixed residential and commercial use in existing communities. The program paired "ecosystem restoration with redevelopment activities to promote mixed-use town centers where people can live, work, and thrive," as TRPA put it. Under this approach, developers could acquire incentives for greater building heights and densities in town centers. They could transfer development rights into the new project from outlying development then retire and restore the donor sites. This goal was an almost complete reversal of forty-plus years of TRPA philosophy that mandated lower density and building height.

The creation of new town centers encompassing mixed uses became popular in California to solve traffic congestion, a lack of available land, and a shortage of achievable housing. The most notable of these is Santana Row in San Jose, California. A similar design created a mixed-use village development at the ski area base in the nearby Olympic Valley. Stacked condominiums overlaid ground floor commercial space with an underground parking garage beneath, and all are within walking distance of the ski lifts.

To reinforce the public/private partnership philosophy, California Tahoe Conservancy Executive Director Patrick Wright and several Basin leaders created a nonprofit organization to raise funds from private and corporate sources in 2010. Under its founding CEO, Amy Berry, the Tahoe Fund quickly identified previously untapped non-governmental sources of capital; it emerged as a critical funding facilitator that filled the gap between large federal grants and the required local contribution. Financially stalled environmental improvement projects became more economically viable.

Despite its successful birth, the regional plan was still at risk in its infancy. Prompted by a Tahoe resident with a grievance over decades of perceived regulatory transgressions, the state of Nevada put TRPA "under the gun" in 2011 with a bill to withdraw from the bistate compact if changes to the agency's plan did not occur. The opponents resurrected an archaic strategy from the grave of the 1970s–1980s playbook of political confrontation, factual misrepresentation, and legal threats. Eventually, Nevada accepted the approved regional plan and did not follow through on its threat. Regional plan approval happened despite U.S. Senators Dianne Feinstein and Harry Reid and Sierra Club's objections. A neighborhood environmental group sued to overturn it. However, a trial court rejected the lawsuit in 2014, and an appeals court upheld the decision the following year.

Once unthinkable and thought extinct at Tahoe, big projects found a newly receptive audience at TRPA. Here, TRPA looked to leverage the enormous profits from new projects to remove dilapidated structures, eliminate pollution sources, expand transit services, increase public access, and restore environmentally damaged lands. After a proposal competition in 2011, TRPA approved two "demonstration" projects that highlighted their new philosophy of melding redevelopment activities with ecosystem restoration to achieve a better economy and sustainable natural environment.

The Homewood Mountain Resort Master Plan [28] would revitalize a struggling ski area with a hotel, village, and residential units. It will roll back development elsewhere and

Homewood Villages architectural rendering [28]. (*JMA Ventures LLC*)

cure the ski area's longstanding environmental problems dating from its construction in the early 1960s. The Boulder Bay project would remove the blighted Tahoe Biltmore Lodge & Casino in Crystal Bay. Replacing it will be an eco-friendly mixed-use resort that reduces polluted stormwater, decreases vehicle emissions, and shifts the site away from gaming dependence. Boulder Bay [43] broke ground on its first phase in 2017. The project has since been acquired by a real estate investment group with demolition of the Biltmore and outlying buildings targeted for 2022 followed by construction of a new hotel casino with a reduced gaming footprint. The Homewood project began work in January 2020 with the replacement of a ski lift. TRPA approved additional projects with similar benefits for the Edgewood Lodge and Golf Course [9] in 2012 and Heavenly Mountain Resort in 2015. Both projects progressed rapidly toward completion.

While planners focused on an environmentally beneficial "look and feel" of the future-built environment, a more considerable environmental risk lurked in the surrounding forests. In 2007, an abandoned campfire ignited one of the worst Tahoe wildfires in recent memory. Unlike Mark Twain's 1861 escaped campfire in Tahoe Vista that harmlessly burned a small area, the Angora Fire [44] scorched 3,000 acres, incinerated 250 homes, and caused $160 million in the destruction of private property, not including lost business and ecological damage. Five years earlier, a discarded cigarette ignited the Gondola Fire that laid waste to 673 uninhabited acres on Heavenly Mountain Resort's eastern flank. These two conflagrations laid bare the effects of the nineteenth-century logging recovery and a century of fire suppression policy on public lands. Dense, overstocked forests were susceptible to intense out-of-control fires that could cause severe environmental damage to the lake.

The memory of the Gondola Fire and the horrific aftermath of the Angora Fire illuminated the urgent need to do more forest fuel treatment by thinning and prescribed burning. Forest fuel reduction became a high priority and attracted U.S. Senator Dianne Feinstein's attention.

Aftermath of Angora Fire showing severcly burned trees and forest floor [44]. (*David C. Antonucci*)

Feinstein focused on planning and funding the environmental improvement projects following the 2007 presidential forum. Tahoe holds a special place in Feinstein's heart, where she visited as a young adult and resided part-time as a lakefront property owner. Feinstein co-sponsored the $415 million Lake Tahoe Restoration Act of 2009, which included funds earmarked for forest health projects. Between 1997 and 2012, over 50,000 acres received forest fuels reduction treatment. The program is ongoing and successful while enjoying broad local support.

Increasing watercraft movement among western lakes brought the specter of harmful aquatic invasive species to Lake Tahoe's waters. Some species such as curly-leaf pondweed and Asian clams had gained a foothold in Tahoe and threatened to spread with disastrous results. In 2008, mandatory boat inspections began, funded as an environmental improvement project and incoming boat owners' inspection fees.

The federal government and the two states refocused on restoring Lake Tahoe's water quality through a total daily maximum load (TMDL) plan adopted in 2010. The plan named the aging transportation infrastructure—roads, highways, and parking lots—as the primary source of clarity reducing pollutants. Under the TMDL plan, the forced reduction in the pollution loading to Lake Tahoe would occur with an interim goal of restoring average annual clarity to 80 feet by 2031, and eventually 100 feet—a figure not seen since 1970. Plan implementation will cause local governments to deal with stormwater runoff into the lake through community storm drain systems. They will carry this out by encouraging the installation of best management practices to control runoff from individual properties, improvement of stormwater

Boat inspection for aquatic invasive species. (*JMA Ventures LLC*)

conveyance systems, and treatment of stormwater before discharge into the lake. In 2017, plan implementation achieved its first five-year milestone of a 10 percent reduction in fine sediment, but the lake has yet to reflect this reduction through consistently improved clarity.

In 2011, the four-year environmental thresholds review breathed relief into Tahoe guardians as it showed that 63 percent of the thresholds were now in attainment status, compared to 19 percent in 2001. Simultaneously, Lake Tahoe's resident population had lost 10,000 people since the 2000 census, presumably because of a rapid run-up in property values in the early 2000s, the Great Recession, and the steep decline in South Shore casino patronage. Many persons cashed out their real estate appreciation and moved to less expensive areas. Later, others lost their income sources due to a slowdown in tourism and construction, forcing a relocation.

In 2012, after measuring the best Secchi disk clarity in ten years at 75 feet, scientists with the Tahoe Environmental Research Center expressed their tentative view that clarity loss may be slowing. Although average annual clarity showed some improvement, summer and nearshore water transparency were still growing concerns (see page 78).

Enabled by improved digital communications methods, grassroots activism began its rise as an expression of citizen empowerment beyond the usual bureaucratic agencies and environmental advocacy groups. Neighborhood watchdog groups such as Friends of the West Shore and the North Tahoe Citizen Action Alliance arose to fight nearby projects approved under the more relaxed development philosophy of TRPA. Pipe Keepers started as a guerilla-style group anonymously monitoring discharges from storm drains and conducting their own Secchi disk measurements. The League to Save Lake Tahoe organized Eyes on the Lake to use citizen surveillance to find invasive species and staged Forest Stewardship events to mobilize citizen volunteers to work on forest health projects.

The Tahoe Environmental Research Center produced a Citizen Science smartphone app that enabled volunteers to see and report water quality conditions around the shoreline.

The quadrennial environmental thresholds evaluation of 2015 showed another incremental improvement with 70 percent of the thresholds in attainment status. That year, clarity measured 73.1 feet—a 4.8-foot decline from 2014, but still 9 feet better than the prior worst year of record in 1997. The year 2017 surpassed the previous record low clarity following unusually heavy runoff that flushed out four years of drought-accumulated sediment in the watershed.

In 2010, the resident (excluding tourists and seasonal residents) population hovered around 55,000 people, about half of the 1964 projection for this period. On an annual basis, the region experienced some 26 million visitor-days, 10 million vehicles prowled the roads, and the area enjoyed a $4.7 billion total economy. In the same year, as measured by the overall boundaries of land affected by development, urbanization covered 10.4 percent of the terrestrial watershed, and 47,400 dwellings units existed.

As part of its effort to encourage the accelerated movement of development rights from undesirable locations to more environmentally sound sites, TRPA embarked in 2016 on an ambitious effort to restructure its development rights transfer program. Development rights include itemized quantities as tourist accommodation units, commercial floor areas, and residential unit allocations associated with existing structures.

Treating development rights as commodities subject to banking, buying, selling, and trading became the fundamental precept. The objective is to optimize the movement of development rights for the benefit of the environment. Going back to Bill Morgan's consensus-building philosophy, TRPA organized a working group of the usual agencies, local governments, business organizations, and environmental interests. In 2018, the group offered its recommendations to streamline the process, simplify transfers across intergovernmental boundaries and reduce fees while adhering to the overall cap on development. Added to these was the proposal to offer bonus residential unit development rights as incentives to build more achievable workforce housing. The TRPA governing board approved the plans in late 2018 without any meaningful opposition.

To return to the "Tragedy of the Commons" analogy, shepherds could now transfer their grazing rights among each other to obtain a better outcome without impacting the Commons grazing pasture. One shepherd could quickly sell his grazing rights in a less productive Commons area to another shepherd through an intermediary. The receiving shepherd could then put these rights to use in a more productive grazing zone without overloading the Commons. Here, the benefits are mutual. The Commons benefits environmentally, and the shepherds gain economically overall.

The sharing economy found its way to the Tahoe Basin early in the second decade of the new century in the form of short-term vacation home rentals run remotely by individuals. Rental of individually owned second homes had always been a part of the Tahoe vacation accommodations scene. Traditionally, local realtors managed these in large pools of houses and condominiums rented out by the week, month, or season. This arrangement changed in 2008 with the debut of internet-based vacation home rental (VHR) apps that allowed individual homeowners to bypass the realtor and deal directly with the customer. The trend shifted the market to more lucrative nightly and short-term occupancies. With this shift came the continuously changing infusion of tourists into formerly quiet neighborhoods populated with locals and seasonal workers and mostly vacant second homes. The noticeable increases in traffic, parking, noise, and overcrowding created a harsh backlash that spurred residents to oppose the new reality vehemently.

Strict ordinances established in 2015 in South Lake Tahoe with fines of as much as $1,000 for excess vehicles did not quell the uprising.

Voters in South Lake Tahoe, where the problem was most serious, turned to the ballot box in 2018 to cure the problem. They narrowly approved proposed new rules phasing out short-term rentals in all except the tourist commercial-zoned areas and dense residential neighborhoods near the casino core. By 2019, other jurisdictions were beginning to regulate short-term rentals, though TRPA still has avoided wading into the controversy as of 2021. In July 2021, Placer County imposed a moratorium on new short-term rental permits because of a crisis-level shortage in long-term workforce rental housing.

Decaying infrastructure, savvy competitors at now year-round ski resorts, and a vibrant Truckee commercial core drove the North Shore in California into a downward economic spiral worsened by the Great Recession of 2008. Desperate to recapture its former leading destination status, the area turned to a business coalition of retail, recreation, and tourist accommodation interests for leadership. The North Lake Tahoe Resort Association and its charismatic and visionary Director of Infrastructure and Community Partnerships Ron Treabess launched into an ambitious Tourism Master Plan update process. A 2 percent room tax allowed the association to fund vital tourism infrastructure projects such as biking and hiking trails, wayfinding signage, visitor information centers, and transportation improvements. In 2018, Placer County took over administering the highly lucrative 2 percent room tax allocation and spending, although this may change to a return of local control to the Resort Association.

In three attempts over twenty-five years, TRPA worked toward a final piece of its comprehensive planning program—the Lake Tahoe Shorezone Plan. The third plan reached completion and obtained governing board approval in 2008. In a throwback to the old combative paradigm, two environmental groups objected to the number of new piers and buoys the plan would allow. The Sierra Club and the League to Save Lake Tahoe filed an action to invalidate the program and won a trial court decision in 2010. An appeals court upheld the decision in 2012, and TRPA admitted defeat.

Following the now tried and true method of consensus building, TRPA in 2015 assembled all stakeholders and urged the parties to work collaboratively toward consensus solutions. The effort was the fourth attempt by TRPA to gestate a shoreline plan that could survive beyond its birth.

The planning group introduced its new shoreline plan in 2018, where it met with the resounding approval of the TRPA governing board and no significant opposition from environmentalists. The new Lake Tahoe Shoreline Plan sets caps on additional piers and buoys, promotes boater education, creates a 600-foot no-wake zone, provides a pathway for marinas to expand, and cracks down on illegal moorings. The plan took effect in 2019, and TRPA held its first new buoy permit lottery and began considering new pier permits in 2021.

In the fall of 2018, at the end of an eight-year study and community involvement process, all involved agencies approved the U.S. 50 South Shore Community Revitalization Plan [34, 37]. The ambitious plan seeks to solve long-standing transportation, environmental, social, and infrastructure problems associated with the Stateline casino core and nearby California properties. The central feature is rerouting through traffic around the casinos on the existing Loop Road and reworking the old Highway 50 casino corridor into a pedestrian-friendly local street. New affordable housing units will replace those displaced by the project and then some. Affected residential and commercial areas will receive infrastructure benefits from new sidewalks, street lighting, bike trails, parks, traffic calming, and transit service. Less traffic congestion, lower air pollution, reduced greenhouse gas emissions, and improved stormwater runoff quality will be among the most critical net environmental benefits.

Multi-use trails have long been a highly desirable and now essential amenity at Tahoe. The first multi-use trail at Tahoe was a 2.2-mile segment built northeast of Tahoe City in 1973 by the Tahoe City Public Utility District. In June 2019, the spectacular 3-mile Tahoe East Shore Trail [45] opened between Incline Village and Sand Harbor State Park. The trail begins by paralleling Highway 28 above the roadway; it then grips the shoreline from the bike trail underpass at Hidden Beach to the state park. Due to its environmentally sensitive location on steep erodible land and scenic shoreline, the total cost was an astounding $12.5 million. A ninety-one-space parking lot at the trailhead alleviates parking demand at Sand Harbor, allows users to walk or bike the distance to the park entrance, and reduces car vs. bike conflicts on the narrow roadway.

Tahoe East Shore Trail [45]. (*Tahoe Fund*)

As the 2020 coronavirus pandemic raged throughout the world, Tahoe was not invulnerable. With the initial spring lockdown in California, tourism dropped sharply. Dire predictions speculated on a 20–50 percent drop in tourism income and estimated 5,000–7,500 job losses in that sector. Tahoe was desolate and the economic outlook bleak for a while—vacant hotels, idle marinas, closed ski areas, empty streets, struggling restaurants, and suffering retail businesses. The League to Save Lake Tahoe speculated that this would be good for the lake's environment, giving it a long-needed chance to heal.

The quiet times were not to last, however. With the lifting of lockdown order, restless people turned to what few options they had for recreation and outdoor experiences. Tahoe became the destination of choice for day trips and longer-term visits. What unfolded was unprecedented tourism volume increase and associated negative environmental impacts.

Federal, state, and local agencies were wholly unprepared to manage and mitigate the demand. Recreation areas became overcrowded, public parking lots overflowed, and daily traffic jams materialized where few had occurred. In the words of one long-time Tahoe local, it was a Fourth of July-sized crowd day after day.

The new visitors' callous behavior angered locals and perplexed governmental agencies as if the overcrowding was not impactful enough. Naïve and careless visitors left mounds of trash and food waste that tarnished beaches, parks, and trailheads and created conflicts with wildlife, especially bears. Large groups packed into residential rental homes, making noise, traffic, parking, and refuse disposal problems.

In 2020, California State Parks saw a 44 percent increase in trash collection volume from the prior years. Many permanent residents feared the increased density and lack of masks, social distancing, and sanitation would lead to more outbreaks of COVID-19 and overburden the medical care system that could not serve the larger population. TRPA opined that it was not the pandemic that caused such problems but exacerbated them and forced them to the forefront.

In South Lake Tahoe, residents protested the influx of visitors with derogatory signs along Highway 50. Others formed online discussion groups to pressure local governments to address neighborhood and the general environmental impacts.

New opportunities for remote work and the restrictive public health measures initiated an exodus of affluent workers and their families from the San Francisco Bay Area. In the aftermath of the COVID-19 restrictions, high demand for residential real estate arose, with buyers bidding against each other and offering all cash, no contingencies purchase terms. Year over year, ending in the second quarter of 2021, increases in sales volume varied between 37 percent for the North and West Shores and 75 percent for South Lake Tahoe. The median sales price jumped 50 to 59 percent in all areas except the East Shore from Glenbrook southward. In nearby Truckee, the new resident influx doubled to 1,000 for 2020, creating a swift population increase of 6 percent.

The dawning of 2021 brought some much-needed science-based good news. In 1970, Tahoe Research Group investigators noted the unexplained population collapse of the native zooplankton *Daphnia* and *Bosmina*. The investigators suspected the introduction of non-native Mysis shrimp and Kokanee salmon or increased algae growth might be the cause.

Above: Mysis shrimp, maximum length: 20 mm. (*UC Davis*)

Right: Daphnia, typical size: 1–5 mm. (*Wikimedia Commons*)

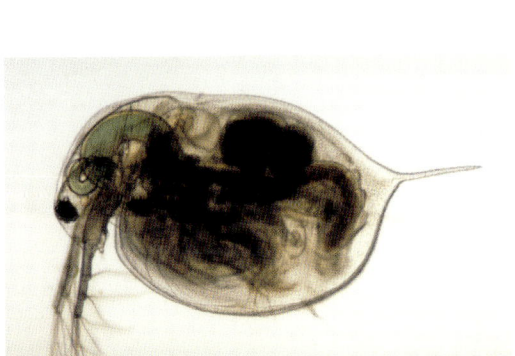

In 2011, investigators discovered an anomaly in Emerald Bay. The occurrence of mysis shrimp had all but disappeared, followed by an explosion in the Daphnia population. After these events, there was a surprising 36-foot increase in water clarity in Emerald Bay.

Scientists postulated that the *Daphnia* were responsible for consuming microscopic algae and suspended fine inorganic particles. They excreted these as dense pellets that sank to the lake bottom.

Mysis shrimp had decimated the *Daphnia*, severely reducing assimilative capacity, the inherent natural ability to handle the lake's pollutant load. However, with the Mysis shrimp absent, the *Daphnia* rebounded, and their feeding clarified the water. Manually removing the invasive Mysis shrimp could allow a rebounded *Daphnia* population to clear the water.

Introducing the Mysis shrimp as a food source for the introduced lake trout raises the question of humans' culpability in tinkering with the aquatic ecosystem. Human-caused watershed disturbance adversely affecting the lake's clarity was already a given.

Not well known until 2011 was that the 1963–65 introduction of Mysis shrimp into the aquatic environment had a considerable impact on lake clarity. Increased amounts of suspended particles and algal growth-stimulating dissolved pollutants entered the lake from human activity. However, they remained much longer in the lake due to the now-absent *Daphnia*.

These findings refer us back to the environmental conflict of the later twentieth century and the debate over the degree of human responsibility for disturbance of the watershed as a significant clarity reducing factor. It raises the question of whether the 1-foot-per-year decline in clarity would have been so dramatic and worrisome. Indeed, other sources such as automotive exhaust and air deposition of blown-in pollutants were affecting clarity adversely. In any event, the clarity loss, albeit less, would have occurred anyway.

UC Davis and University of Nevada researchers proposed removing Mysis shrimp by trawling at night when the shrimp are surface feeding and processing the haul into a dog treat to offset costs.

In this case study, we see the principle that the ability of humans to change the environment exceeds their ability to foresee and willingness to concern themselves with the impacts of these changes. This lack of awareness and economic incentive to act has been the case for much of Lake Tahoe's human and environmental history. Fortunately, science was ready to intervene with practical answers.

Transportation continued to be on TRPA's front burner in April 2021. The increase in vehicle traffic was an issue with congestion, air quality, and air deposition of fine particles and nitrogen compounds from engine exhaust into the lake well into the automobile tourism era. For most of TRPA's history, the transportation problem—primarily expressed as the congestion and pollution-inducing vehicle miles traveled (VMT)—has remained its nemesis. Unlike clarity loss which has at least slowed, transportation continues to worsen.

Past land-use restrictions curtailed new highways and expansion of existing roadways to stop overdevelopment. However, population growth outside the Tahoe Basin and the resulting change in visitation increased VMT, exacerbating the prevailing traffic conundrum. Tahoe could not just "road-build" itself out of this box.

To solve the challenging transportation puzzle called for a new tactic. The 2020 Linking Tahoe: Regional Transportation Plan/Sustainable Communities Strategy offered innovative solutions. Within a twenty-five-year implementation period, the $2.4 billion plan will initiate projects and programs that address a range of transportation solutions.

One major project is executing transit systems connecting town centers and recreation destinations and neighborhoods and town centers. Other strategies are using technology to disseminate better travel information, such as parking availability and additional multi-use trails, including a bikeway circumnavigating Lake Tahoe. The plan would engage all solutions to connect communities, the workforce, employers, and recreation sites using a methodology focusing on these site-specific needs. It is as if TRPA placed its first footstep into the next era of a transformed Tahoe.

In 2020, a group of altruistic and motivated SCUBA divers began a project to clean up the 75.1 miles of nearshore lake bottom along the shoreline. After scouring the 66 percent of the lake bottom along 49.5 miles of shoreline the group plucked 20,453 lb in 2020 and 2021. Significantly, 10.5 percent of this weight was plastic that degrades into fine particles that interfere with the ecosystem.

On the heels of the 2021 lake bottom cleanup effort, the California Sportfishing Protection Alliance reached a court settlement with Pacific Bell to remove an abandoned telecommunications cable. The 8 miles of underwater cable contains an estimated 120,000 lb of lead that was dissolving into water.

With the memory of the disastrous Angora Fire still fresh in the minds of nervous locals, an unimaginably worse threat emerged on August 30–31, 2021. The Caldor Fire began as a relatively small incident on August 14 near the small town of Grizzly Flats, El Dorado County and over 28 airline miles from the western edge of the Tahoe Basin. A convergence of adverse factors contributed to the rapid expansion of the fire—two consecutive dry years including the third driest in the 127-year period of record, high winds, hot temperatures, and years of neglect of fuels build up in the region's forests.

The fire was the second of only two fires to cross the summit of the Sierra Nevada. The fire raced eastward down the slope below Echo Summit, jumped across the Christmas Valley residential area, skirting South Lake Tahoe, and ravaging its way to the western boundary of Heavenly Mountain Resort. One can only credit the years of forest and urban fuels reduction projects in Christmas Valley and the heroic actions of firefighters that no structures or lives were lost.

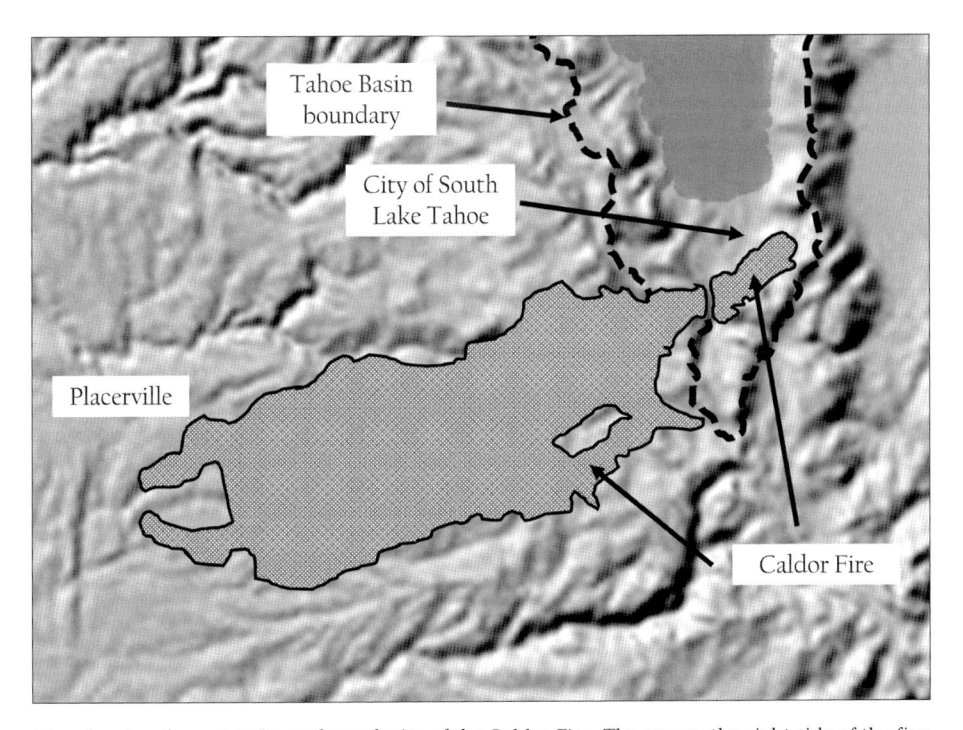

Map showing the approximate boundaries of the Caldor Fire. The gap on the right side of the fire footprint is Christmas Valley, Lake Tahoe Basin. Here, the winds pushed the fire eastward, but previous forest fuel reductions and firefighters' heroic actions prevented the loss of structures on the valley floor.

The fire was not declared contained until October 21, 2021. Its legacy was 221,835 acres burned and 1,003 structures destroyed. In the Tahoe Basin, roughly 10,400 acres burned, but no structures were lost.

The aftermath of the fire will require substantial long-term recovery efforts to reduce hazardous trees, stabilize and revegetate burned areas, mitigate bulldozer carved fire breaks, and repair trails and backcountry roads. Preliminary post-fire studies determined that water quality and clarity were not significantly impacted after the weeks of smoke, ash fall, and runoff from an October 24 atmospheric river storm.

As we noted in discussion of an earlier era, climate change has been penetrating the Tahoe environment insidiously for the last 100 years. However, it has only been since 1968 when intensive environmental monitoring began that lake scientists began to realize what they were seeing was the unmistakable signature of climate change. The body of data revealed alarming trends related to increased air and water temperatures. Warming of air and water means less precipitation falls as snow, the lake mixes to lesser depths, peak streamflow increases, high and low lake levels become more extreme, and drought conditions intensify.

None of this is good for Lake Tahoe. This era began on the ash heap of environmental conflict and, like a phoenix, rose from the ashes to resurrect and then reinvent itself. The lack of progress in reversing the lake's decline and fixing the ailing economy forced once warring parties to cooperate and even collaborate. It became an urgency for environmentalists and a matter of survival for business interests. The result was a new form of self-governance that leveraged the combined strength of formerly dissonant parties within the framework of mandatory regional planning and oversight.

For the first time, all stakeholders viewed the Tahoe Basin as their "commons" and understood the zero-sum realities of self-interested actions. To put it more frankly, the environmentalists begrudgingly accepted development and business growth as the vehicles to pay for the ecological improvements they desired. Business and property rights groups understood they would be the economic engine for funding environmental projects and programs. It was as if the shepherds had agreed that the health and sustainability of the grazing commons was the fundamental goal, and each shepherd had an obligation to honor and contribute toward this mutual objective.

11

Tahoe Beyond the Present

Foreseeing the future is dicey and almost always off the mark. For this reason, we consider here an imagined future rather than a predicted future. We can examine existing conditions and extrapolate local, regional, and global trends to create possible future scenarios, however likely. The overarching trend is how the final resolution of the Tahoe Conflict will play out. From these starting points, we visualize a future one can only imagine.

Over the short term, the new residential development rate should remain stable and begin a long-term steady reduction that will span many decades. With only 4,000 vacant parcels remaining in 2013, the Tahoe Basin may reach full residential buildout on available land by 2033. After full buildout, existing residences will become even more valuable, and redevelopment may bring new vitality to these old structures.

As the stock of vacant commercially zoned land remains low and expensive to develop, attention will focus on revitalizing existing commercial and tourist accommodation development. TRPA may reinforce this approach with a policy that rewards revitalization of existing development over entirely new projects on undisturbed ground. The shift toward renewal of existing projects will result in an overall lower level of urbanization under the TRPA strategy to create town centers that lower the development cap in exchange for higher density pockets. The long-term outcome should be reduced sprawl, compact mixed-use urban hubs, more efficient movement of people, and improved aesthetics of the surrounding landscape.

Led by the U.S. Forest Service, the two states, and the surrounding counties, the process of performing remedial projects that restore damaged lands will continue. Privately funded redevelopment activities that acquire valuable development rights from impacted areas and complete restoration of the donor sites will significantly repair ecological damage. These should be successful in reversing the pollution load into the lake.

South Lake Tahoe casino gambling hotels that depend mainly on drive-up clientele have declined since 2000 and show no signs of reversing this long-term trend. They are falling victim to age, shrewd competitors, and changing market conditions. The use of these properties in the future may change as they become less viable. The government may buy their sites and restore them to natural conditions. The property owners may replace or repurpose them with less impactful projects incorporating a much smaller gaming footprint like the Boulder Bay project. These new projects will embrace a sustainable business model and function more in harmony with the traditional outdoor spirit and geotourism theme of the Tahoe experience.

The reliance of the economy on tourism will have to change for two reasons. Tourism dependence limits resilience to adverse external factors such as recessions, pandemics, and fuel shortages. Also, the trend is downward for short-term gaming-related visitation. The solution will lie in diversification into other areas such as light manufacturing, digital commerce, recreation, remote work, software development, cultural centers, healthcare and wellness, and environmental innovation, to name a few.

We may see regional rollback programs that remove undesirable, obsolete, and under-performing residential and commercial developments and restore these sites. These acquisitions will be the first steps in a grand scheme over the long term to reduce the presence of humans and move the Tahoe Basin toward a modern national park-like condition.

The repatriation of the Washoe tribe may accelerate with culturally significant pieces of federal and state lands transferred back into tribal control. This process will allow them to recapture, keep alive, and educate their descendants about tribal history and culture. The opportunity for a Washoe living history demonstration facility may present itself. The Washoe could demonstrate aspects of their traditional ways to educate non-Native American visitors about their history, culture, and philosophy of sustainable living.

Just as short-term app-based rentals trend rapidly in Tahoe, so will other occupancy types. The next logical phase after short-term rental occupancy may be short-term second homeownership. Commonly known as shared ownership or timeshare, it is not new to Tahoe, having arrived at the Brockway Springs Resort in 1972. In the years after, timeshares at Tahoe emerged as conversions of existing motels, apartments, condominiums, and a few new builds on commercial land.

The difference in the future will be applying this concept to single-family detached dwellings in residential neighborhoods. This nascent industry characterizes this movement as the "democratization" of second home ownership. Traditional timeshares only grant purchasers a right to occupy for a defined interval for a fixed period. The "democratized" co-ownership model for second homes conveys an actual ownership interest in the house to two or more parties. The trend will bring along all the negative impacts previously associated with the VHR and the short-term rental situations in the 2010s.

Inevitably, limits on daily user occupancy will become mandatory to prevent Tahoe from being "loved to death." Increased population growth in the surrounding multistate region and innovations that intensify occupancies, such as VHRs and shared ownership, will drive the need for a fixed limit.

Past unsuccessful efforts in the 1970s considered a basin user fee for funding environmental improvement projects and using market forces to cap the number of tourists. The intense local unpopularity of both daily limits and user fees thwarted the implementation of either. In contrast, the National Park Service and other land management agencies extensively use these techniques to attenuate visitor numbers to heavily impacted parks and recreation areas.

A critical difference between national parks and the Tahoe Basin is the ownership and occupancy of private property in the Tahoe Basin. This circumstance does not generally or widely exist in national parks. Also, impeding interstate travel is another challenge unique to Tahoe. How agencies manage user fees, private property access, and interstate movement will be matters of constitutional interpretation.

The continued population growth in California and Northern Nevada and ensuing pressures on Tahoe will necessitate a Tahoe Basin population limit. Indeed, in the wake of the massive 2020–21 pandemic visitation surge, TRPA acknowledged that the pandemic did not cause these visitor impacts but instead directly aggravated existing problems.

The unhealthy forest that is the legacy of nineteenth-century logging and twentieth-century fire suppression policies must be solved to avoid a catastrophic wildfire conflagration. This process is already underway but must be accelerated. This program is heavily dependent on public funding since the removed trees have little or no economic value. The development of innovative technology can help recover some costs, such as the clean burning of logging waste for energy production and reuse of woody material for restoration and conservation projects.

Global climate change will exert its effects in ways that bring challenging to foresee changes throughout the Tahoe Basin ecosystem. Despite our best efforts to restore the watershed, the lake may still degrade for reasons beyond our immediate control due to rising air and water temperature and precipitation and runoff regime changes in the watershed. We can look to a future of hotter summers and greater extremes in weather events. Less frequent and shallower mixing of the lake will mean declining clarity. More intense drought will mean more frequent wildfires and smoke events in the watershed, die-off of wildlife habitat, and desiccation of wet meadows. Communities and the regional economy may face a shorter winter sports season. On the upside, we may see a more extended summer season, although with impacted boating due to lower lake levels—not a bright picture of this aspect of the future.

We can be confident that transportation will look radically different. It must change since the current transportation system is dysfunctional and a significant deficiency for the environment and the business and recreation sectors. We can look to other mountain communities that developed more recently and downplayed the car as the transport method of choice. Their effective public transit networks can be any combination of the transit planner's adage, "fast, free, fun, and frequent."

Housing for the Tahoe workforce will have to resolve in favor of workers. The shift of single-family housing toward short-term rentals in the 2010s, newly resident remote workers, and the run-up in real estate prices put extra strain on local workforce housing. The solution will lie in collaboration across the spectrum—environmental agencies, local governments, large and small employers, advocacy groups, and developers—under the umbrella of a basin-wide organization. A myriad of solutions will present themselves, including new workforce housing complexes inside and outside the basin, conversion of existing structures such as casinos, rental incentive programs for second homeowners, mass transit of workers into Tahoe from nearby areas, housing assistance programs, and employer-owned housing.

What about the return of the Olympic Winter Games? A persistent business and government alliance centered on Reno's dreams of returning the Olympic Movement to the region. After unsuccessful bids for the 1998 and 2002 Winter Games, the Reno Tahoe Winter Games Coalition remains focused on producing a successful bid, likely well into the 2030s and beyond.

As a minimum, any Winter Games event must result in a net improvement in the economic, social, and environmental quality of the Tahoe region. Earning the broad support of the affected communities will be essential. It must restitute and guarantee the modern winter sports facilities promised in 1960 but never realized.

The return of the Winter Olympics might offer an exceptional opportunity. The infusion of funds can create effective transportation solutions such as rail service, spur redevelopment of decayed commercial cores, and provide achievable housing. A post-Olympic Tahoe should be the beneficiary of a renewed and vibrant winter sports economy that adds ice and sliding sports facilities and dispersed human-powered outdoor recreation to supplement existing winter resorts and activities.

The wildcards in shaping the Tahoe of the future are the positive effects of advanced technologies that have yet to reveal themselves. These fall into stormwater runoff treatment innovations, alternative transportation options, watershed remediation techniques, electronic environmental surveillance and monitoring, and artificial intelligence. Future land use and environmental regulation decisions may occur with the assistance of the cold, objective logic of artificial intelligence in place of human reasoning and politics.

In its finality, the Tahoe Conflict will likely resolve on the side of environmental protection. Though profit motive and individual benefit forces will not go extinct, plans and policies are in place to blunt them or channel them into more environmentally sound alternatives. The public benefit philosophy may fully prevail and firmly root itself in the planning and regulation policies that will govern Tahoe into the distant future.

If this next era were to have a name, we might call it "Transformed Tahoe"—transformed as in a dramatic and positive change in all aspects of Tahoe's natural and human environments. This era embraces an enlightened philosophy of preserving natural resources tied to a sustainable human presence and a resilient local economy.

Looking into the far distant future, Tahoe may well transcend many of its past setbacks and achieve its true destiny as a futuristic national park-like commons surrounded by a few low-impact, mixed-use communities and compact residential areas. We might tag this era as "Back to the Future" Tahoe. One meaning of "Back to the Future" as an expression is "what is old is new again," i.e., recycling the nostalgic features of the summer season destination tourism era forward into this new era. The earlier era's desirable characteristics of low population density, superior lake clarity, mass transportation, and a comfortable outdoor experience will prevail again. What will differ is its affordability, the persistence of past development, and inclusion of a four-season economy. Absent will be intense high-rise casino hotels, aggravating traffic jams, and outdoor destinations overrun with tourists.

Consider this as an innovative hybrid national park with private inholdings. These inholdings would be consolidated, constrained in expanse, and prohibited from increasing the intensity of use. The National Park Service would manage the balance of the Tahoe Basin outside of the private inholdings as some form of national park designation. The possible categories are national recreation area, national monument, national preserve, national scenic area, or national lakeshore, all with specific restrictions applicable to Tahoe. TRPA would continue to oversee the activities within the private inholdings. Public access to private littoral lands below the high-water mark in Nevada may occur by legislation or court mandate. This scenario may be as close as Tahoe can reach a complete national park-like condition in the next 100 years.

Perhaps, we can look to the stakeholders involved in the TRPA Pathway 2007 process who expressed the most optimistic outcome of the Tahoe Conflict in their upbeat and captivating vision statement for the condition of the Tahoe Basin twenty years hence:

> [T]he lake is clear and blue, the Basin's communities have sustainable economies and a variety of neighborhoods that benefit from a healthy forest and Lake clarity, the Tahoe Basin has a diversity of convenient transportation options that enhance the travel experience and lower congestion with less environmental impact, [and] there are a wide range of recreational opportunities and choices that feature the natural beauty and ruggedness of the Basin while protecting it for future generations.

Perhaps.

BIBLIOGRAPHY

Atkins, K., "Variability in periphyton community and biomass over 37 years in Lake Tahoe (CA-NV)," *Hydrobiologia* (2021)

Bailey, R. G., *Land Capability Classification of the Lake Tahoe Basin, California-Nevada: A Guide for Planning* (South Lake Tahoe: U.S. Department of Agriculture, Forest Service, 1974)

Balance Hydrologics, Inc., *Polaris + Pomin Wetland Restoration Feasibility Study* (South Lake Tahoe: Tahoe Resource Conservation District, 2020)

Benson, L. V., *et al.*, "Holocene Multidecadal and Multicentennial Droughts Affecting Northern," *Quaternary Science Reviews* (2002), pp. 659–682.

Braun, C. L. and Smirnov, S. N., "Why is Water Blue?" *Journal of Chemical Education* (1993), pp. 612–614.

Britton, L. J., Averett, R. C., and Ferreira, R. F., *An Introduction to the Processes, Problems, and Management of Urban Lakes* (Reston: U.S. Department of Interior, Geological Survey, 1975)

Bureau of Reclamation, *Truckee River Operating Agreement* (Washington, D.C.: Bureau of Reclmation, 2008)

California Department of Water Resources, *Annual Inventory of Water Use Lake Tahoe and Truckee River Basins Calendar Year 2018* (Sacramento: California Department of Water Resources, 2019)

California Tahoe Conservancy, *Tahoe Climate Adaptation Primer* (South Lake Tahoe: California Tahoe Conservancy, 2021)

Chandra, S., Segale, H., Wittmann, M., and Adler, S., *Species of Lake Tahoe's Aquatic Food Web* (Incline Village: Tahoe Environmental Research Center, 2010)

Clean Water Team, *Color of Water Fact Sheet* (Sacramento: State Water Resources Control Board, 2010)

Cobb, D., "How the Southern Pacific Saved Lake Tahoe," *Sierra Sun* (April 16, 2021), p. 19.

Congress of the United States, *Truckee-Carson-Pyramid Lake Water Rights Settlement Act, Title II Of P.L. 101-618* (Washington, D. C.: U.S. Government, 1990)

Cotruvo, J., *Contaminant of the Month: Drinking water aesthetics* (January 1, 2016), watertechonline.com/water-reuse/article/15549869/contaminant-of-the-month-drinking-water-aesthetics

DeCourten, F., "Geology of the Lake Tahoe Region," *Lecture Series* (Olympic Valley, California: Squaw Valley Insitute, April 2005)

Domagalski, J. L., Morway, E., Alvarez, N. L., Hutchins, J., Rosen, M. R., and Coats, R., "Trends in nitrogen, phosphorus, and sediment concentrations and loads in streams draining to Lake Tahoe, California, Nevada, USA," *Science of the Total Environment* (2021), 141815-.

Fogerty v. State of California (1986), Civ. No. 25115 (Court of Appeals of California, Third Appellate District, November 24, 1986)

Free, C. M., *Ancient Lakes of the World* (February 9, 2020), web.archive.org/web/20200218125019/https://marine.rutgers.edu/~cfree/ancient-lakes-of-the-world/

Gardner, J. V., Mayer, L. A., and Hughs Clarke, J. E., "Morphology and processes in Lake Tahoe (California-Nevada)," *Geological Society of America Bulletin* (2000), pp. 736–746.

Gertler, A. *et al.*, "Local air pollutants threaten Lake Tahoe's clarity," *California Agriculture* (April 2006), pp. 53–58.

Griffin, L., "Lake Tahoe could get clarity in murky times," *Sierra Sun* (March 31, 2020)

Jacobs, M., *CalTopo, USGS, NZ Topo* (2020), caltopo.com/map.html#ll=39.10582,-119.89655&z=11&b=t.

Kauneckis, D., Koziol, L., and Imperial, M., "Tahoe Regional Planning Agency: The Evolution of Collaboration," in *Environmental Governance in Watersheds: The Importance of Collaboration to Institutional Performance* by Imperial, M. T. and Hennessey, T. (Washington, D.C: National Academy of Public Administration, 2000)

Kumar, R. R., "A Comparison of Basalt Fibre with that of Basalt (Rock) for a Composite Application," *International Journal of Engineering Research in Mechanical and Civil Engineering* (2017), pp. 86–89.

Lake Tahoe Nearshore Science Team, *Definition of Lake Tahoe's Nearshore Zone* (Albany: U.S. Forest Service, Pacific Southwest Research Station, 2013)

LakeNet, *Ancient Lakes* (2004), worldlakes.org/lakeprofiles.asp?anchor=ancient; *Deepest Lakes* (2002), worldlakes.org/lakeprofiles.asp?anchor=deepest; *Lake Profile Tahoe (USA)* (2004), worldlakes.org/lakedetails.asp?lakeid=8498; *Largest Lakes (Area)* (2002), worldlakes.org/lakeprofiles.asp?anchor=area

Lienhard, J. H., *The Timber Square Set* (2003) uh.edu/engines/epi1901.htm

Marchetta, J., "Getting Serious About Transportation," *Tahoe Regional Planning Agency* (April 16, 2021), trpa.gov/getting-serious-about-transportation/

Mariner, R. H., Presser, T. S., and Evans, W. C., *Hot Springs of the Central Sierra Nevada* (Menlo Park: United States Geological Survey, 1977)

McGaughey, P. H., Eliassen, R., Rohlich, G. A., Ludwig, H. F., and Pearson, E. A., *Comprehensive Study on Protection of Water Resources of Lake Tahoe Basin Through Controlled Waste Disposal* (Al Tahoe: Lake Tahoe Area Council, 1963)

Moonshine Ink Staff, "If not Tourism, Then What?" *Moonshine Ink* (April 14, 2021)

Moonshine Ink, *Tahoe Talks—If Not Tourism, Then What?* (Truckee, California, April 5, 2021)

Nathenson, M., *Chemistry of Lake Tahoe, California-Nevada, and Nearby Springs* (Menlo Park: United States Geological Survey, 1989)

National Park Service, *Convergent Plate Boundaries—Accreted Terranes* (February 11, 2020), nps.gov/subjects/geology/plate-tectonics-accreted-terranes.htm#:

Nearshore Science Team, *Lake Tahoe Nearshore Evaluation and Monitoring Framework* (Albany: USDA Forest Service Pacific Southwest Research Station, 2013)

Nevada Division of Water Resources, *Truckee River Operating Agreement 2018 Water Use Inventory* (Carson City: Nevada Department of Conservation and Natural Resources, 2019)

NOAA Office of Coast Survey, *Electronic Navigation Chart for Lake Tahoe* (Silver Spring, Maryland: National Oceanic and Atmospheric Administration, 2021)

Orona, J., "Truckee Grapples with Urban Flight Influx," *The Union* (March 2, 2020), theunion.com/news/truckee-grapples-with-urban-flight-influx/.

Regional Planning Partners, *Tahoe Basin Regional Vision Summary* (Stateline: Tahoe Regional Planning Agency, May 2007)

Reno Tahoe Winter Games Coalition, *About Us—Who We Are* (May 10, 2021), renotahoewintergames.org/.

Richards, R. C., Goldman, C. R., Frantz, T. C., and Wickwire, R., "Where have all the Daphnia gone? The decline of a major cladoceran in Lake Tahoe, California-Nevada," *Internationale Vereinigung für Theoretische und Angewandte Limnologie: Verhandlungen* (1975), pp. 835–842.

Romero, E. D., *An Economy Dominated By Tourism, Tahoe Region Still Feeling Impact From First Stay-At-Home Order* (December 18, 2020), capradio.org/articles/2020/12/18/an-economy-dominated-by-tourism-tahoe-region-still-feeling-impact-from-first-stay-at-home-order.

Rozak, B., "Tahoe Biltmore to host last hurrah before demolition begins," *Tahoe Daily Tribune* (April 15, 2022), pp. 1, 25.

Rundel, P. W. and Millar, C. I., "Ecosystems of California," in *Ecosystems of California* by Mooney, H. and Zavaleta, E. (Oakland: University of California Press, 2016), pp. 613–634.

Rush, F. E., *Bathymetric Reconnissance of Lake Tahoe, California and Nevada* (Carson City: Nevada Division of Water Resources, 1973)

Safipour, S., interview by Linda Adkins, *2020–21 North Lake Tahoe Real Estate Market* (March 4, 2021)

Sahoo, G. B., Schladow, S. G., and Reuter, J. E., "Hydrologic budget and dynamics of a large oligotrophic lake related," *Journal of Hydrology* (2013), pp. 127–143.

Schladow, G., Toy, A., and Watanabe, S., *State of the Lake Report* (Incline Village: Tahoe Environmental Research Center, 2020)

Schladow, G. *et al.*, *A Tahoe Mysis Control Plan* (Incline Village: UC Davis Tahoe Environmental Research Center and University of Nevada Reno, 2021)

Shiffer, Z., *A Short History of Short-Term Rentals in California* (March 25, 2019), kqed.org/news/11734283/a-short-history-of-short-term-rentals-in-california.

Sierra Sotheby's International Realty, "Home market demand continues to outpace supply at Lake Tahoe," *Tahoe Daily Tribune* (July 16, 2021), p. 25.

Simpson, G., *Roof Pendants of the Sierra Nevada* (2013), sierra.sitehost.iu.edu/papers/2013/simpson.html.

Smith, K. D. *et al.*, "Evidence for deep magma injection beneath Lake Tahoe CA-NV," *Science* (August 27, 2004), pp. 1277–1280.

Sunman, B., *Spatial and Temporal Distribution of Particle Concentration and Composition in Lake Tahoe, California-Nevada* (Davis: UC Davis, 2004)

Tahoe Environmental Research Center, *Climate Science* (April 14, 2022), tahoe.ucdavis.edu/climate-change; *Lake Clarity Tracker* (June 3, 2021), clarity.laketahoeinfo.org/Results/Detail/WaterClarity#

Tahoe Environmental Research Center, *State of the Lake* (Incline Village: UC Davis, 2021)

Tahoe Regional Planning Agency, *Lake Tahoe Nearshore Evaluation and Monitoring Framework—Phytoplankton* (February 7, 2018), laketahoeinfo.org/NRAPFinding/Detail/22

Tahoe Regional Planning Agency, *TRPA 2006 Threshold Evaluation* (Stateline: Tahoe Regional Planning Agency, 2007)

Tahoe Transportation District, *US50/ South Shore Community Revitalization* (February 25, 2021), tahoetransportation.org/projects/us50-southshore-community-revitalization/

Taylor, K., *Investigation of Near Shore Turbidity at Lake Tahoe* (South Lake Tahoe: Lahontan Regional Water Quality Control Board, 2002)

Thodal, C. E., *Hydrogeology of Lake Tahoe Basin, California and Nevada, and Results of a Ground-Water Quality Monitoring Network, Water Years 1990–92* (Carson City: U.S. Geological Survey, 1997)

TRPA Staff, *Staff Report: Adoption of the 2020 Linking Tahoe: Regional Transportation Plan/Sustainable Communities Strategy* (Stateline: Tahoe Regional Planning Agency, 2021)

Twain, M., *Roughing It* (Hartford: American Publishing Co., 1872)

United States Geological Survey, "Lake Tahoe and Vicinity (map)" (August 1895); *Map Products* (2001) URL no longer active; *USGS 10337000 LAKE TAHOE A[T} TAHOE CITY CA* (May 20, 2021), waterdata.usgs.gov/nwis/dv?; *What is Hydrology?* (May 18, 2021), usgs.gov/special-topic/water-science-school/science/what-hydrology?qt-science_center_objects=0#qt-science_center_objects

WalletInvestor, *Tahoe House Price Historical Chart (Placer County)* (March 27, 2021), walletinvestor.com.

Waring, G., *Springs of California* (Washington, D.C.: United States Geological Survey, 1915)

Watanabe, S., Vincent, W. F., Reuter, J., Hook, S. J., and Schladow. S. G., "A quantitative blueness index for oligotrophic waters: Application to Lake Tahoe, California–Nevada," *Limnology and Oceanography: Methods* (2015), pp. 100–109.

Weisstein, E. W., *Stadium* (February 21, 2022), mathworld.wolfram.com/Stadium.html.

Whaley, S., "Tahoe bike path carries high construction cost," *Las Vegas Review-Journal* (March 20, 2016)

Wikipedia Foundation, *List of lakes by depth* (April 23, 2021), en.wikipedia.org/wiki/
List_of_lakes_by_depth; *List of lakes by volume* (March 14, 2021), en.wikipedia.org/wiki/
List_of_lakes_by_volume.

Wkimedia Foundation, *Ancient lake* (April 21, 2021), en.wikipedia.org/wiki/Ancient_lake.

Wolfram Research, Inc., *Stadium* (2021), mathworld.wolfram.com/Stadium.html

INDEX

ABOUT THE AUTHOR

DAVID C. ANTONUCCI has resided in the Lake Tahoe area for over forty-seven years. He received bachelor's and master's degrees in civil and environmental engineering from California State Polytechnic University and Oregon State University and is a licensed civil and environmental engineer. His professional career started in 1973 and included senior manager and policy-level positions in the public sector. He oversaw water pollution enforcement at Lake Tahoe for the Lahontan Regional Water Quality Control Board between 1975–1980. For seventeen years, he managed a special district in Tahoe City responsible for water, sewer, parks, and recreation services.

He currently serves as president of the Sierra Nevada and Olympic Winter (SNOW) Sports Museum and on the North Lake Tahoe Historical Society board. Antonucci lectures on Lake Tahoe history and natural science at the UC Davis Tahoe Environmental Research Center.

He enjoys studying the science and environmental issues and the natural history of Lake Tahoe. Antonucci is currently working on his next book, *The Geology of Lake Tahoe*.

He has done original research that has identified the Lake Tahoe travel route and camp-sites of Mark Twain and published the book *Fairest Picture: Mark Twain at Lake Tahoe*. His book *Snowball's Chance: The Story of the 1960 Olympic Winter Games* won a 2009 book award from the International Ski History Association. He regularly gives multimedia presentations to visitors and conference groups on Lake Tahoe's natural history interpretation, Mark Twain at Lake Tahoe, and the 1960 Olympic Winter Games. To arrange speaking engagements and book signings, please visit his website www.tahoefacts.com.

The author enjoys cross-country skiing, snowshoeing, mountain, road and winter fat biking, flatwater kayaking, hiking, and RV camping. He resides in Tahoma, California, with his spouse, Jenny Antonucci.